Hellfires of Grief

Love Poems

C. Eldon Taylor

Hellfires of Grief: Love Poems

©2013 by C. Eldon Taylor

All rights reserved. No part of this book may be reproduced in any form or by any means, electronic or mechanical, including photocopying, recording, or by any information storage and retrieval system, without written permission except in the case of brief quotations embodied in critical articles and reviews.

ISBN: 0615814662
ISBN-13: 978-0615814667

LCCN: 2013909042

Printed in USA
by CreateSpace

Published by
C. Eldon Taylor
Henrico, Virginia 23228

Introduction

Hellfires of Grief: Love Poems is a collection of 222 poems written after the disembodiment of my beloved Carol Susan on October 31, 2011. I use the word *disembodiment* rather than the word *death* or *death to the body* since my beloved's beautiful radiant spirit left her physical body to return to the spirit realm. The words in my journals were inadequate to express my experiences of loss, grief, and despair. I converted the raw words of grief in my journals into poems to express in words the language of my tears, broken heart, and the hellfires of grief.

Tear's Words
poems
my grief concentrated
what my tears say when I listen
my tears insisted I translate them into words
inspiration from my soul
soul's blood
been said tears are healing
if tears are healing
perhaps tear's words
may be healing too

It is my hope, wish, and intent sharing the tears of grief translated into words brings others a measure of comfort and healing energy to all who read them.

Namaste

C. Eldon Taylor

Hellfires of Grief:
Love Poems
Table of Contents

1977   Page
Carol Susan   March 27, 1977   1

2011
Uroboros: Nov 19   2
Love Is In the Air: Nov 19   4
Memorial Service: Nov 22   5
Dreaming Dragons: Nov 22   8
Hour of Remembrance: Nov 22   9
Journaling: Nov 22   10
Crying in Bathroom: Nov 22   12
Denying Impermanence: Nov 23   14
Regret and Remorse: Nov 23   18
C Word: Nov 23   20
Alchemical Crucible: Nov 23   22
Golden Cocoon: Nov 24   24
Often Enough: Nov 24   26
Grow Old With Me: Nov 24   28
Thanksgiving 2011: Nov 24   30
CS's Memorial Stone: Nov 24   32
Burning Incense: Nov 25   33
Caregiver Distress: Nov 26   34
C-PAP Machine: Nov 29   36
My Tail: Nov 30   37
Proportions: Dec 2   38
Ceremonies: Dec 4   39
Stages Cycles of Grief: Dec 4   40
Special Chairs: Dec 7   42
Scouring Installment Plan: Dec 9   44

Kali: Dec 10	46
Going First Left Behind: Dec 12	48
The Shrine: Dec 13	49
Storm Clouds: Dec 17	50
Expanding Shrine: Dec 19	52
CS's Christmas Card: Dec 19	55
Holiday Traditions: Dec 19	56
Memories: Dec 19	57
WRONG!: Dec 21	58
Dates On Your Urn: Dec 21	60
Blue Blue Christmas: Dec 25	61
Christmas 2011: Dec 25	62
Great Circle: Dec 26	64
Recovery Higher Purpose: Dec 31	66

2012

Hellfires of Grief: Jan 1	**68**
New Years 2012: Jan 1	70
Dehydration: Jan 2	72
Despair Golden Dreams: Jan 5	73
You Miss Her Too Much: Jan 7	76
Special Spoon: Jan 12	77
Tiger Balm: Jan 13	78
Lunar New Years Cards: Jan 22	79
Lunar New Year 2012: Jan 22	80
Always and Forever: Jan 30	82
Soulmates Journey: Feb 1	83
Chakra Energy Connections: Feb 19	86
Grief CD: March 16	91
Widower: March 21	92
Grief Work: March 20	94
Disembodiment: March 27	95
Priorities: March 22	96
Old People Couples: March 24	98
New Restaurant: March 29	99
Three Great Events: April 2	100

Home: April 4	101
Easter 2012: April 8	102
Materialize Catching Up: April 13	104
Get On With It: April 15	106
Heart Break: April 22	107
Six Months: April 29	108
CS's Birthday 2012: May 8	110
National Shrine: May 12	112
Mother's Day 2012: May 13	114
34th Wedding Anniversary: July 30	116
Nine Months: July 31	117
First I Ching Together: July 31	118
Soul Lessons: Aug 13	120
New Circumstances: Aug 13	121
My Birthday 2012: Aug 20	122
Gifts: Sept 20	124
Enough: Sept 30	125
Shining Moment: Oct 4	126
Beyond: Oct 13	127
Negative Thoughts: Oct 14	128
Clean Towels: Oct 15	129
A Dragon Named Grief: Oct 31	130
Black Mola Dress: Nov 2	132
Forgiveness: Oct 29	137
Assimilating the Dragon: Nov 11	138
Life Review: Nov 12	140
"Dead Woman Walking: Nov 22	142
Carnival Rides of Grief: Nov 23	144
Holidays Are Hell: Nov 23	145
Paradox of Love: Nov 26	146
Soul Food: Nov 26	147
Masters Naturally: Nov 28	148
Quest: Nov 30	149
too subtle: Nov 29	150
Surrounding Grief: Nov 30	151

Eyes of Love Eyes of Loss: Dec 6	152
Grounding First: Dec 2	154
Ten Thousand Things: Dec 6	155
Holiday Season: Dec 10	156
Invisible Earthquake: Dec 11	157
Abandonment: Dec 13	158
Little Creature: Dec 13	160
Mothering the Little Child: Dec 13	162
Grief Spiral: Dec 16	163
your little creature: Dec 15	164
Night Journey: Dec 21	166
Return Visit: Dec 22	168
Return Visit II: Dec 22	170
Piercing the Veil: Dec 21	172
Holidays at Our Cottage: Dec 23	173
Mirror Message: Dec 24	174
Snake Oil: Dec 31	176
Your Awareness: Dec 27	178
New Traditions: Dec 29	179

2013

Portal to Your Soul: Jan 1	180
Inexhaustible Grief: Jan 1	181
New Year 2013: Jan 1	182
Crying: Jan 2	183
Telling Carol Susan: Jan 2	184
Rewriting My Story: Jan 2	186
Dark Mother: Jan 6	189
What Does Healing Look Like: Jan 5	190
Moon Cycles: Jan 6	192
Negation and Mystification: Jan 6	193
Carnival Rides of Grief II: Jan 6	194
Shared Dreams: Jan 6	195
Missing My Kitten: Jan 7	196
Your Head On My Shoulder: Jan 7	198
Kittens at the Shrine: Jan 9	199

Loss: Jan 9	200
Love's Shadow: Jan 9	201
Screensaver: Jan 9	202
Magic Herbs: Jan 20	203
Puppy Food: Jan 13	204
Grief's Blood Soul's Blood: Jan 13	206
My Teacher: Jan 15	208
No Accidents: Jan 19	210
Old Coat: Jan 23	212
Lilith & Snakie Compassion: Jan 27	214
Lilith's Daughter Son: Jan 27	216
One Day: Jan 26	217
One Day II: Jan 26	218
My Healing: Jan 28	220
Our Wedding Picture: Jan 30	221
Family Hugs: Feb 1	222
Garden Time: Feb 2	224
I Know Very Little: Feb 3	226
Shrine Balance: Feb 8	228
Lunar New Year: Feb 10	230
Day of Disembodiment: Feb 10	232
Double Rainbows: Feb 10	233
High Impact Lessons: Feb 10	234
My Spirit Valentine: Feb 13	235
Patience: Feb 13	236
Two Candles Two Flames: Feb 21	237
Grief and Grieving: Feb 26	238
Memories II: Feb 26	240
Compound Grief: Feb 27	241
Withered Up: March 3	242
Spirit Realm Embrace: March 3	244
Precious Possessions: March 6	246
Sacred Clutter: March 4	248
Two Peas in a Pod: March 11	249
Grief & Golden Angel: March 11	250

Bitter Pills: March 4	252
Grief & CW: March 8	253
Grief Transformation: March 13	254
I Knew You As A Child: March 13	258
Time and the Mystic: March 14	259
Five Hundred Days: March 17	260
Last Dance: March 19	262
On Assignment: March 16	264
Carry Your Luggage: March 19	265
Hidden Mysteries: March 19	266
A Few Pitiful Poems: March 22	269
My Higher Self: March 20	270
Heart of My Heart: March 22	272
Paradox of Loss & Grief: March 23	274
Tear's Words: March 23	276
Golden Joy: March 26	277
Withered Up Old Dragon: March 26	278
Destination: April 1	281
Experience: April 1	282
Love: April 5	285
Superficial: April 5	286
Dream Details: April 7	287
Two Kinds of Seeing: April 9	288
Shocked: April 10	290
Transformational Magic: April 10	291
Spirit Vision: April 12	292
New Memories: April 13	296
Little Things: April 14	297
Two Modes of Existence: April 14	298
Eighteen Months: April 15	299
Healing Journey: April 21	300
Failed Hero: April 24	304
Trio of Sad Days: April 25	306
Celestial Princess: April 24	308
Eighteen Months II: April 27	309

Birthday Present 2013: April 27	310
little irrational: April 28	311
Sweet Sweet Attention: April 28	312
Sweet Sweet Attention II: April 28	313
Missing Physical Being: April 29	314
Energy Bodies : April 30	316
Looking Back & Beyond: April 29	319
My Grief and I Ching: Jan 10	320
My Quest and I Ching: March 3	321
My Path and I Ching: July 31	322
Making Room: May 1	323
Making Room II: May 3	324
Golden Cocoon Waiting: April 30	326
Healing Broken Hearts: May 3	327
Making Room III: May 4	328
Make the Best of It: May 4	329
Fresh Eyes New Eyes: May 4	330
Making the Best of It: May 5	331
Inspiration: April 6	332
Poems and I Ching: Feb 17	334
Gone Not Gone: April 30	335
Hellfires of Grief II: April 25	336
Carol Susan March 27, 2013	**338**
Quotations Appendix	340
Copyright Permissions	348
Acknowledgements	349
Author	350

Carol Susan

numinous power of the Feminine

natural expression of mysterious Yin ways

primal archetypal image of Woman

essence of flowering lotus

enchanting mythological princess

beautiful daughter of Tara

transformation's Divine Vessel

from you I see my changing

you guide by being you

you are also changing

we are becoming friends

C. Eldon Taylor
March 27, 1977

Uroborus

when we met came together
we talked about mythic images
symbols speaking without words
one of our favorites is the tai chi
fish coiled together
yin yang
female male
dark light
together create unity
I made a large tai chi
wall hanging
matching bedcover
symbols of our unity
two become one

another favorite image is the uroborus
coiled serpent "eating" its tail
tai chi dragon image
union of male female energies
create one
power to regenerate
eternal image
birth rebirth

Carol Susan had my wedding ring
custom made in the shape of the
uroborus
half rose gold half yellow gold
I never take it off

we collected other images of uroborus
often talked about them
enjoyed sharing mythic images
ancient symbols
alchemical images
I Ching images

when Carol Susan started her business
she selected a purple Asian uroborus as her logo
symbolize her dream of increasing connectedness
unity
later had her logo made into a mola bag
carried it for many years in her work
symbol of her dream to increase connectedness
kindness compassion love unity
the purple uroborus mola bag is part of the shrine
now

I look at my uroborus wedding ring
Carol Susan had custom made for me
symbol of our union
soulmates
yin yang
dragon version of the tai chi
the uroborus transforms
regenerates
symbol of immortality
symbol of our union
soulmates
always forever and beyond

November 19, 2011 eulogy
transcribed March 7, 2013

Love is in the Air

few days before she disembodied
Carol Susan ate wonton soup
and a fortune cookie
as was our tradition
I always gave her half my fortune cookie too
Carol Susan told me she was full
put my fortune cookie aside
day after she disembodied
when I saw the fortune cookie
needed to open it
it said

"Love is in the air"

early message from my beloved
glad to get the special message
fortune cookie
reminding me
her love is in the air
always has been
already knew
could always feel her love
I still can
I always will

from eulogy November 19, 2011
transcribed January 25, 2013

Memorial Service

you requested your memorial service be scheduled
three weeks after your disembodiment
provide time for Panama family to
make travel arrangements
scheduled Saturday November 19, 2011
Taryne Jade and I collaborated on
writing your obituary
designing your memorial card
selecting pictures to accompany the
music you selected
285 pictures of your life
our life together
birth until towards the end
celebration of your life in music and pictures
sad painful labors of love
I cried selecting the pictures
listening to the music
thinking about what a memorial service means
I did not want to have a memorial service
I did not like what a memorial service means

we selected a black marble urn
to hold your ashes
your ashes were returned in a
plastic box from the crematorium
had a plaque created for the urn
engraving will be done later
selected a picture for enlargement
2 by 3 feet
first two were unacceptable
third represented your spirit well enough
as well as pictures are able to
memorial service unacceptable

since I did not like what that meant

DeVaney Wong families few close friends
gathered Friday night at the cottage
for barbeque

the day of the memorial service
Taryne Jade and I selected six dozen purple irises
placed them with the guest book at the entrance
two large bunches on either side of the urn
in front of your picture
Taryne Jade welcomed everyone
we started with eulogies
Taryne Jade went next to last
very powerful loving tribute
from her heart to her dragon mother
her mother's daughter
she remembered how you gave eulogies
she wanted to do the same for you
sad painful labor of love
my eulogy was last
focused on your life of love
compassion caring helping others
at the end I ask everyone to give you a
standing ovation for a life well lived
I learned that from you

Kuan Yin White Tara Mother Mary were present
Kali was too
while I did not talk about Her presence
Her presence was hard to ignore
it was a memorial service after all
I did not like what that meant

the next day family close friends gathered
at the cottage for Chinese food from
your favorite Chinese restaurant in Richmond

owner expressed his condolences
always made you your favorite soup
it was not on the menu
ordered hot and sour soup
Peking duck crispy duck
chow fun beef dry
moo shu pork
served passion fruit sorbet
set around the table all day
telling stories remembering you
all wanted copies of the memorial CD
glad I had 30 made

Taryne Jade created a memorial web site
excellent creative professional job
sad painful labor of love

I am sorry we needed to have a
memorial service memorial web site
I do not like what that means
I know you liked the memorial service
you were present along with the
goddesses ancestors others
Taryne Jade invoked your presence for her eulogy
you were there with her
surrounding her with your golden love
looked like she was in the arms of a golden angel
she was of course
her golden rainbow dragon mother
surrounding us all

November 22, 2011 Journal I
transcribed March 28, 2013

Dreaming Dragons

I dreamed I was a butterfly
or was I a butterfly dreaming
I was a person dreaming
I was a butterfly

no matter as I am
a dragon dreaming
I am a person dreaming
I am a dragon
you are a dragon too

when you were ill
I would tell you
I wanted us to come back
as dragons next time
they have much longer
life expectancy
you smiled and nodded
you understood the message
you know
we have been dragons
together all along
always
forever
and
beyond

November 22, 2011 Journal I
transcribed March 4, 2013

Note: My thanks to Chuang Tzu for the dreaming butterfly image

Hour of Remembrance

monday 5:50 pm you disembodied
I set aside 5 to 6 pm every monday
hour of remembrance
special incense black candles
many mondays
I lay in our bed
beside where you used to be
cried talked to you
then I set in your special chair
talked to you cried
wrote in our journal cried
hour of remembrance
67 weeks
now I write in our journal
talk to you cry

monday hour of special remembrance
my remembrances are ongoing
hourly
weekly
monthly
and
beyond
all are special
some golden
some rainbow colors
some black
all are special

November 22, 2011 Journal I
transcribed February 14, 2013

Journaling

I felt compelled to write
about the disembodiment
of my beloved Carol Susan
I could not find the journal
she gave me in 2002
I bought one just like it
except for her inscription
the new inscription is different
in part it says
"welcome to the hellfires of grief"
I started 11/22/11
22 days after
my beloved Carol Susan
disembodied
her beautiful and radiant
soul left her body

December 31, 2011
I started to write
directly to my beloved
pouring out
my heart and soul

I write in our journal
every day
all the words
I could ever write
will not be enough
to express my love
for my soulmate

while I know
Carol Susan's physical eyes
cannot read my words

I know
her spirit
eyes do

she looks over my shoulder
as I write in our journal
sometimes she does not like
the words
but rarely complains

all the words
I have written
help a little

Carol Susan's
reading
over
my
shoulder
helps
more
than
words
can
ever
say

November 22, 2011 Journal I
transcribed January 12, 2013

Crying in the Bathroom

near the end when Carol Susan
was not doing well
she would tell me it was OK to cry
we cried together from time to time
after the diagnosis
surgery reoccurrence
we mostly focused on treatments
hopeful for cures healing
later when we cried together
crying caused Carol Susan
additional pain
when I started to cry she did too
so I blocked out some of my tears
choked then down
swallowed my grief
I cried mostly in private
Carol Susan knew
she would ask me if I was
crying in the bathroom
I would say
no of course not
we both knew that was untrue
sometimes I would say
well maybe a little
we both knew that was not true either
I did not want to add to her pain
an act of loving kindness
act of love
Carol Susan understood
she knew I was crying in the bathroom

we both had anticipatory grief
started with the diagnosis
even before that we both had
a vague sense of foreboding
several years of weird symptoms
without a diagnosis or treatment
dark shadow surrounding our lives

after my beloved disembodied
I released the swallowed tears
cried myself to sleep
cried as I awoke
cried in my sleep as I would awake
with tears in my eyes
perhaps I cried in my dreams
I did not remember them
I even cried in the bathroom

during the first few months
after her disembodiment
after a particularly intense
bout of crying
I would tell Carol Susan
see I'm crying now
making up for lost time
she would surround me with her love
glad I was not holding back my tears
she still is

November 22, 2011 Journal I
transcribed March 24, 2013

> Life and death are of supreme importance.
> Time passes swiftly and opportunity is lost.
> Let us awaken.
> awaken….
> Do not squander your life.
>   Zen Night Chant

Denying Impermanence Urgency

Carol Susan long maintained
she would not live into old age
she expected to die before she got old
I did not want to believe
so I denied her intuition
pretended she would grow old with me
while she wanted to she knew better
I acted as if we had all the time in the world
she indulged me in my denial
because she loves me

Carol Susan talked about her sense
of the finiteness of life
sense of urgency
her wish to live life to the full
she was acutely aware
of the impermanence of life
would tell me life is short
not to postpone put off delay
she called it her high definition life

I did not want to acknowledge your urgency
your awareness of the impermanence of life
I did not live with a sense of urgency

sense of the fragility of life
life's impermanence
I took life somewhat for granted
I squandered time
lost opportunities
oh I talked about death as my advisor
just behind my left shoulder
more head than heart
Carol Susan practiced what I
mostly talked about
I was busy denying
the reality of your wisdom

I am very sorry and ashamed
I did not take your words more seriously
unwilling to accept your awareness
of your impermanence
need for urgency
now I ruminate about how I wasted time
squandered time

my coming into awareness
that you were correct
awful awakening
your disembodiment
worst experience of my life
now I experience regret remorse
sorrow grief
hellfire and dark nights
wishing I had not squandered time
wishing I had celebrated
with you more often
expressed my appreciation
thankfulness more often

held you more tightly more often
not ever let you go
I am sorry
I know with your loving compassionate
caring ways
you have forgiven me
my shortcomings and imperfections
we lived an intense life
shared the intimacy of soul mates
yet I know I could have done better
I could have acknowledged
your sense of impermanence
fragility of life
your intuition
not squandered time
pretending it was not finite
your disembodiment
awful way to learn
experience the reality
of life's impermanence
fragility
finiteness

I am doing better at acknowledging
my limitations imperfections
I am not looking backwards
quite as much
not ruminating about squandering time
quite as much
I am not exactly looking towards the future
I am living each day
looking into the beyond
my opportunity to awaken
while still embodied

in the spirit realm

I know each physical life is impermanent
fragile finite
your disembodiment
the most painful lesson of my life
I know your beautiful radiant spirit left
your physical body to return to the
spirit realm
where I visit in golden dreams

while I squandered time
denied your mortality
your intuition
your urging we live life with
a greater sense of urgency
looking back over thirty four years
we lived a very intense life
golden cocoon
golden alchemical crucible
sharing the intimacy of soulmates
while not comparable to my higher self
that old alchemist Carlos Eldon
I did the best I could within my limitations
I know you said it was good enough
I heard you
the old alchemist agrees

November 23, 2011 Journal I
transcribed March 24, 2013

Note: Zen Night Chant quoted from
Joan Halifax. *Being with Dying: Cultivating Compassion and Fearlessness in the Presence of Death.*
Boston: Shambhala, 2009, page 196.

Regret and Remorse

when I remember
certain things
I am filled
with regret
and
remorse

errors of commission
regrets for words spoken
regrets for actions taken
remorse for staying in my head
not my
heart

errors of omission
regrets for words not spoken
regrets for actions not taken
remorse for staying in my head
not my
heart

memories dark and painful
too late now to change
at least the memories
I work towards
self forgiveness
for
being human flawed
led astray from
the path with heart

when the dark energy
does not fade
I look at pictures
taken during happy times
remember
the energy of
love

when all else fails
I read the golden dreams
they shine bright with love

regret and remorse fade
for a while

as
love
continues

Always
Forever
and
Beyond

November 23, 2011 Journal I
transcribed November 26, 2012

C Word

when my beloved
was first diagnosed
I could not say
the word "cancer"
very primitive defense
saying the
word "cancer"
makes it real
not saying means
it does not exist
magical thinking
forced myself
to say "cancer"
hated hearing
my saying
the word
"cancer"
hated the word
"pancreatic"
even more
looked at
numbers
worse cancer
worse mortality rate
shortest life expectancy

sadly my magical thinking
did not work
perhaps I
should have never said
the word "cancer"
my head knows
magical thinking is a
primitive defense
my heart knows
magic is real
sadly my magical thinking
did not work
not the same as
magic

perhaps
I did not
believe
hard
enough

November 23, 2011 Journal I
transcribed March 12, 2013

Alchemical Crucible

golden alchemical crucible
two rainbow bodies
fire of love
male female
yin yang
fire of love
burns impurities
rough edges
imperfections
fire of love
intense experience
burning impurities
transforming into gold
pure unity

one of the rainbow bodies
disembodies
leaves the golden crucible
transforms to spirit
leaving the remaining one
a different transformation
golden crucible turns black
fire of love becomes
hellfires of grief
intense heat
impurities
burning and burning

know my beloved did not
completely leave the crucible
transformed into
subtle spirit
yet the crucible turned black
hellfires of grief
turning the crucible black
know the black crucible
conceals the golden one
continue the alchemical work
grief work
purification
burning and burning
hellfires of grief
turning the black crucible
back into gold

November 23, 2011 Journal I
transcribed March 13, 2013

Golden Cocoon

we met   touched
created a cocoon of golden energy
very powerful energy
even when physically apart
together in our golden cocoon
chakras merged
wonderful experience
wonderful energy
beyond words
talked about it anyway
best experience
my beloved agreed
loved the image too

forming our
golden cocoon
returned home
together again

my beloved disembodied
felt half our cocoon
was gone   missing
large hole ragged edges
wounded like me
other half broken raw bleeding
did not know how to heal
our golden cocoon
tried to repair with memories
not the same
mostly added tears grieving

realized the broken part
is my heart
golden cocoon not damaged

my beloved's side not empty
only different
life force transcended
light from our golden cocoon
seems less intense
decided to create
images of our golden cocoon
before and after
at first my beloved's side seemed
empty
then I realized
light reduction due
to looking with
physical eyes
adjusted my vision
see my beloved's
subtle spirit energy
painted the images
my spirit eyes can see
diminished life force
chakras dysfunctional
no reduction in radiance
problem with my spirit sight

even with
diminished spirit sight
I know our golden cocoon
transcends realms
exists beyond time
very powerful energy
even when physically apart
together in our golden cocoon
created by love
soulmates spiritmates
always forever and beyond

November 24, 2011 Journal I
transcribed March 5, 2013

Often Enough

I did not tell you I love you
often enough
I did not tell you I would marry
you again and again
often enough
I did not kiss you
often enough
I did not hold you
often enough

I did often
tell you I love you
would marry you
again and again
kiss you
hold you
nothing seems like often enough
now

I still tell you I love you
I still tell you I would marry you
again and again
nothing seems like often enough
now

now that I can only
hold and kiss you
in my dreams
nothing seems like often enough
not even in my dreams

oh there are things
that are more than
often enough
missing you
darkness
blackness
dark nights of the soul
hellfires of grief
burning and burning
more than enough impurities
more than enough darkness
plenty enough of those
plenty enough of
missing you

November 24, 2011 Journal I
transcribed February 16, 2013

Grow Old With Me

soon after we came together
Carol Susan gave me
a heart shaped seed
that said
"Grow Old Along With Me
The Best Is Yet To Be"
I have always treasured the
grow old with me seed
stayed on the grandfather desk
for 34 years

I moved the
grow old with me seed
to the shrine
accompanied by lots of tears
Carol Susan did not grow old
in her physical body
she disembodied at 57

I wish with all my heart
we could have grown old
together in our physical bodies

the grow old with me seed
is a sacred treasure
a promise from my beloved

Carol Susan
is still along with me
the form of her being

                is
            different
        she is beyond time

        I am growing older
          with her along
    I know the best is yet to be
        I have had glimpses

      I wish with all my heart
     we could have grown old
    together in our physical bodies

        I am growing older
          with her along
    I know the best is yet to be
        I have had glimpses

                            November 24, 2011 Journal I
                            transcribed January 15, 2013

Thanksgiving 2011

we had a simple breakfast
not elaborate like Thanksgivings past
planted ten dozen purple winter pansies
Carol Susan always liked them
ate a small pizza for lunch
not very hungry
talked about the elaborate
Thanksgiving feasts
we used to have
Carol Susan loved to make
Thanksgiving special
family and friends
elaborate table wonderful meal
grief counselor said we were raw
too raw for holiday celebrations
we were not hungry
remembered more than ate
thankful we had Carol Susan embodied
with us as long as we did
center of our family
I do not remember what we had for dinner
know it was not turkey
I was not hungry

Thanksgiving 2011
twenty four days
after our beloved
Carol Susan
disembodied
not like the Thanksgivings
we remembered
worst Thanksgiving
of my life

November 24, 2011 Journal I
transcribed March 21, 2013

Carol Susan's Memorial Stone

Carol Susan loved to visit
Lewis Ginter Botanical Garden
visiting in early February 2011
she requested
a memorial stone
after she was gone
made me sad
through my tears
I managed to agree
after Carol Susan disembodied
her stone was engraved
placed on a path
I visit the garden
now and then
Carol Susan's stone
remember other walks
tell Carol Susan
"see I remembered"
she is pleased
I honored her request
I am glad I could
sad I needed to
I visit the garden
now and then
remember other walks
better walks

November 24, 2011 Journal I
transcribed January 28, 2013

Burning Incense

I burn incense all day most all night
large quantities
first thing upon awakening
last thing before sleep
burning incense to assist
you ascend to a wonderful place
incense not necessary

I send my love with the smoke
message I am thinking of you
I like to watch the smoke rise
towards the spirit realm
soothes my heart and soul
sending my love with the smoke
I know you do not need the incense
you experience my love without it
I know you like it anyway

I only burn a little incense now
ceremony soothes my heart and soul
when will I stop burning incense
perhaps when I can follow the smoke
to the spirit realm
perhaps not even then
I am comforted by the smoke
sending my love to you
know you are too
so I will keep burning incense
comforted by the smoke
soothes my heart and soul
sending my love to you

November 25, 2011 Journal I
transcribed February 7, 2013

Caregiver Distress

I was glad I could be your caregiver
sad you needed one
horrified you needed one
heartbroken you needed one
you were always so
fiercely independent
doing
mothering others
caring loving
acts of loving kindness
guide therapist
teacher coach
facilitator
mentor to many
center of our family
spoiled me
I spoiled you a little too
but you were the master

then the dark times
you needed help
I gave you all I have with love
as your health faded
you needed more care
I gave you all I have with love
glad I could be your caregiver
sad you needed one
horrified you needed one
heartbroken you needed one
I gave you all I have with love
"within my limitations"
as you would say

"within my limitations"
is not about care giving
it is about healing
I did not have the
skills
talents
gifts
to help you heal
your physical body
nor did any one

I have no regrets
about my care giving
glad I could be your caregiver
sad you needed one
horrified you needed one
heartbroken you needed one

heartbroken I could not
help you heal
or find someone else
who could

I am glad you let me be your caregiver
I gave you all I have with love

November 26, 2011 Journal I
transcribed January 17, 2013

C-PAP Machine

I hate my c-pap machine
Carol Susan was concerned about my
snoring and breathing
ask me to get a sleep study
I put it off
then she became ill
her sleep easier disrupted
sleep study sleep apnea
stopped breathing 50+ times/hour
c-pap machine
continuous positive airway pressure
blows coldish air
could not use c-pap machine
facing my beloved
blew cold air on my beloved
turned it on at the last minute
off as soon as awakened
curl up with my beloved
I hated my c-pap machine
blew cold air on my beloved

since my beloved disembodied
I still use my c-pap machine
do not have to worry about
blowing cold air on her any longer
wish with all my heart and soul I did
each time I turn on my c-pap machine
I remember
another sad reminder
my beloved's physical person
is no longer here
I hate my c-pap machine

November 29, 2011 Journal I
transcribed February 2, 2013

My Tail

one day not long ago
I was telling Maya
the story of my tail
how the doctors
cut it off
right after I was born
they did not tell my parents
I have always missed my
physical tail
stored in a jar in the
bowels of the hospital
"baby taylor tail"
I have always known
I have a tail
because the doctors
only knew how to
cut off the physical one
Maya was not overly impressed
by my story
as she can see my tail
you can too
you have always liked my story anyway
we are kittens
after all

kittens always recognize
their love ones

November 30, 2011 Journal I
transcribed January 19, 2013

Proportions

love and grief
are proportional
more intense love
more intense loss
more intense grief
hotter fire
longer burn

basic law
of the universe

I thought
I understood
now I know

it
can
not
be
any
other
way

December 2, 2011 Journal I
transcribed January 9, 2013

Ceremonies

ceremonies provide
some comfort
if only a little
honor you
our love
time together
memories

anger
you are no longer
here to make more
memories
instead I re-live
our life together
and cry
some more

I miss you so much
our world broken
in half
half of me has gone
with you
the other half is
raw and bleeding
damn it all
to hell

December 4, 2011 Journal I
transcribed January 12, 2013

Stages of Grief
Cycles of Grief

stages of grief
misleading intellectual concept
linear thinking
the experience of grief
is not stages
like steps up and out
grief is organic
cycles spirals
that repeat
not pretty spirals
ugly messy
spirals
rough raw
leaking bleeding
turning twisting
tumbling
on and on

stages of grief
march up the steps
in a straight line
get on with it
get over it
get on with your life

cycles of grief
drop ever deeper
body mind emotions
into the heart
soul
center of being

stages of grief
sounds neat
tidy
grief just ain't
that way
don't let anybody
tell you
it is

grief cycles
ugly messy
raw bleeding
spirals
repeating often
that go
on and on

any resemblance
to stages
is purely
coincidental

December 4, 2011 Journal I
transcribed January 12, 2013

Special Chairs

near the end of his embodiment
Carol Susan's father came to stay with us
Carol Susan purchased an electric recliner chair
since she suspected her father
would be too weak to operate the manual type
we brought the chair home
just before he came
he was too weak to ever use the chair
we named it Jim's chair

near the end of her embodiment
Carol Susan was having trouble
getting up from Jim's chair
she requested an electric reclining chair
that raises to standing
I special ordered her chair
it showed up the day after
Carol Susan disembodied
I named it Carol Susan's chair
placed it at the shrine
her physical eyes never saw
her special chair
she never used it

I use Carol Susan's chair
all the time
setting at the shrine
remembering
reading
writing

crying
while Carol Susan watches over me

it is a comfort to set in
Carol Susan's special chair
I know she watches over me

I have been told
I cannot ask for a special chair
I respond I already have two
they are more than enough
too much some times
often too much

both chairs are black
seems proper somehow

December 7, 2011 Journal I
transcribed January 16, 2013

Scouring on the Installment Plan

after the disembodiment of my beloved
my intent was to
"scour my heart out with honest sorrow"
retirement gave me time
grieving gave me distance from all
but a few
plenty of opportunity
too much motivation
even then my scouring has been
on the installment plan
neither my mind or body would allow
a monster abreaction
too many defense mechanisms
too much armor
defense mechanisms in the
service of the ego
scouring on the installment plan
memory by memory
image by image
tear by tear
minute by minute
hour by hour
day by day
week by week
month by month
year by year
on and on

temporarily forgetting she is gone – again
remembering she is gone – again
over and over
scouring on the installment plan

no matter how much I know about
death and dying
grief and grieving
from years of study and work
it helped very little
when it was my turn
to experience the loss
of my beloved
so all my ideas about scouring
were overshadowed by the reality
of my experience
scouring on the installment plan

so I have decided scouring
on the installment plan is OK
just as well since
my body and mind
will not allow
it any other way
scouring on the installment plan

I continue to honor my intent
"to scour my heart out with honest sorrow"
It is just that I am
scouring on the installment plan

I do not know any other way

December 9, 2011 Journal I
transcribed January 23, 2013

"to scour my heart out with honest sorrow" page 192
Joan Halifax. ***Being with Dying: Cultivating Compassion and Fearlessness in the Presence of Death***. Boston: Shambhala, 2009.

Kali

Robert Bly suggests replacing Snoopy
with Kali at the Mall of America
so everyone who looked upon Her
would be "a tiny bit more adult"

I was enchanted with the idea
told Carol Susan if we won
a large lotto prize
I would commission
a large statue of Kali
place it on a hill overlooking I95
as a public service
to help everyone mature a little
Carol Susan smiled not enthusiastic
about the idea
she had experienced Kali up close
while my fascination was intellectual
Carol Susan knew the terror of Kali
giving with one hand
eating with another

when my beloved disembodied
I came to know Kali
at the level of my heart in my center
I am no longer fascinated but
terrorized by Kali's devouring ways
I no longer want to commission
a large statue of Kali

I do not like Kali
She does not care

now I have met Kali up close
am I "a tiny bit more adult"
perhaps
but I do not care

December 10, 2011 Journal I
transcribed November 27, 2012

Robert Bly "How Kali Belongs in the Malls" page 69
Robert Bly and Marion Woodman. ***Maiden King: The Reunion of Masculine and Feminine.*** New York: Henry Holt and Company, 1998.

Going First-Left Behind

you always said
you did not want
to be the last to leave
the one left behind

you
did
not
have
to
leave
so
soon

you could
have stayed
another
ten years
twenty years
thirty years
since I promised
to stay until age 87

now I do not know
why

December 12, 2011 Journal I
transcribed December 26, 2012

The Shrine

shrine to Carol Susan
has images and statues
of
Kuan Yin
White Tara
Mother Mary
Goddesses of Compassion
Carol Susan is Their daughter

no image or statue of
Kali
but She is there
She likes the black marble urn
holds the physical remains
of my beloved
Carol Susan
while Kali is invisible
Her presence is
overwhelming

I do not like Kali
She does not care

December 13, 2011 Journal I
transcribed November 27, 2012

Storm Clouds

for years we saw dark clouds
storm clouds
intense storm
in the distance
they got closer
your health
became more
uncertain
then
horrible disease
black storm clouds overhead
severe lightening
the black hurricane of
pancreatic cancer
then
eye of hurricane overhead
you disembodied
your beautiful and radiant soul
left the physical world
storm resumed even
worse than before
anticipatory grief and mourning
became
grief and mourning
black clouds
intense storm
severe lightening
no silver lining
in sight

we both saw the storm coming
tried all we know to avoid the storm
nothing worked

worse storm of my life
no silver lining
in sight

December 17, 2011 Journal I
transcribed January 23, 2013

Expanding Shrine Memory Walls

started with the black marble urn
ashes of my beloved's physical body
large portrait from memorial service
memorial cards guest book
three black candles
perpetually blooming purple orchid
wedding picture
25th anniversary picture
favorite portraits age 15 and 18
my picture from 1977
Taryne Jade's first portrait
statue of White Tara
Green Tara thangka
White Tara thangka
Gold Tara thangka
statues of Kuan Yin
Mother Mary
grandmother's stone
grandmother's statue of Mary and Jesus
Chinese coins Panamanian coins USA coins
added pictures from childhood
adolescence young adulthood
memory wall
pictures when we first met
added large pictures
wedding picture
25th anniversary
portrait of us from 2009
picture together 2011

ran out of wall

started another wall
wall of lasts
last pictures
Christmas 2010
birthdays 2011
last pictures together
Carol Susan and me
family of three
very sad wall
added more pictures
happy times together
ran out of walls
memory walls
over 50 pictures
the shrine room
very intense experience
comforting and sad
sacred shrine
sacred room

I bring objects to the shrine
to show Carol Susan
I know it is unnecessary
comforts me
does no harm
Carol Susan likes the shrine
even though it is cluttered
comforts me
does no harm

many visitors find the shrine room
too intense

comforts me
setting in the special chair at the shrine
surrounded by memory walls
sharing memories with my beloved
sending love
feeling love
returned

on special occasions
I pour cognac in a special glass
sip a bit leave the rest at the shrine
for my beloved and the goddesses
they drink very slowly
savoring the offering
of my love
sending love
in return

the shrine honors
disembodied soul of my beloved
my soul as well
feeds both our souls
we both know
the real shrine is within my heart and soul
the physical shrine is ever expanding
the real shrine is too
sharing memories with my beloved
sharing golden dreams with my beloved
sending love
feeling love
returned

December 19, 2011 Journal I
transcribed February 14, 2013

Carol Susan's Christmas Card 2011

December 19th
one of Carol Susan's friends
sent me an envelope
before we moved Carol Susan
gave her some books
later taking out a book a card fell out
Christmas card Carol Susan had
picked out for me
two little Boynton cats
"Merry Christmas to My Best Friend"
signed "Love CS"

we gave each other Boynton cat cards
starting in 1977
many holiday celebrations
often the same card
used Boynton cat tags
on our presents in 1977
our first Christmas
converted them to ornaments
on the tree every year
thirty four Christmases

though disembodied
Carol Susan
sent me a special Christmas card
our thirty fifth Christmas
Christmas 2011
only card on display
wonderful message
from my beloved

December 19, 2011 Journal I
transcribed March 21, 2013

Holiday Traditions

we established a wealth of

holiday traditions

each celebrated to the full

now holidays

are not the same

I

observe

remember

I

do not

continue our

holiday traditions

I

have

memories

December 19, 2011 Journal I
transcribed December 27, 2012

Memories

some say memories are bitter-sweet
others say sweet turning bitter
most of my memories are
lovingly sweet
with a hint of salt
often from my eyes
always in my heart
a few are sour and bitter
most are golden sweet
silver sweet like moonlight
starlight
some are rainbow sweet
filled with love
I chose not to focus on the
sour and bitter memories
sometimes they show up
uninvited
your physical person and mine
will generate no new memories
together
so the gold silver rainbow
memories
we share
will have to be enough
most of my memories are
lovingly sweet
I am blessed to have them

December 19, 2011 Journal I
transcribed December 29, 2012

WRONG!

WRONG! JUST DAMN WRONG!
injustice prevails
no merit to being
one of the kindest
most loving caring
yet to be taken ill
suffer die at 57
Mother in her Kali aspect
face of chaos
image of chaos
blue black Bitch
with sharp teeth
eating Her children
as fast as She bears them
where the hell were the
goddesses of compassion
Mother Mary Kuan Yin Tara
when all of this
was going on
taking a nap
on vacation
Kali tricked Them
into the cellar
locked Them in
so She could caper about
stealing my beloved
ruining my life
I wanted more of the
Mother Mary years
Kali could show up
in old age like

She is suppose to
why don't those silly Bitches
play by the rules
humans should get their
threescore and ten
not fifty damn seven

December 21, 2011 Journal I
transcribed January 13, 2013

Dates On Your Urn

took your black marble urn to be engraved
left your ashes at home in the box
they came in from the crematorium
when we went to pick up
your newly engraved urn
they ask if your name and dates were OK

I thought to myself your name is OK
your birth date is OK
your disembodiment date never OK

I answered yes everything is correct

your disembodiment date will never be OK

took your newly engraved urn home
in another sad ceremony
placed your ashes
in your newly engraved urn
placed your urn in the
center of your shrine

your disembodiment date will never be OK
2031 or 2041 would be OK not 2011

your disembodiment date will never
be OK to me

December 21, 2011 Journal I
transcribed March 25, 2013

Blue Blue Christmas

Christmas 2011
without you
in your physical body
thirty-four Christmases together
every time I went shopping
every store
within a few minutes
the song
Blue Christmas
would appear
weird coincidence
I would tear up
acknowledge how true
how awfully true
then entering a store
wondering how long before
Blue Christmas
would appear
within a few minutes
synchronicity at work
one day I heard
our daughter humming
Blue Christmas
quietly to herself
yes it will be
for all of us

it was

December 25, 2011 Journal I
transcribed March 15, 2013

Christmas 2011

first Christmas we are not together
embodied
since
Christmas 1977
I spent the day like most other days
remembering crying raw with grief
I often look at the picture of you
reaching out to me
Christmas 2010
our last Christmas together
in our physical bodies
essence of your loving ways
always makes me cry
I feel your wonderful love
breaks my heart to remember
we will not make more memories
together in our physical bodies
I hold the Christmas card from you
came just the other day
crying feeling your love surround me
I read the Caring Bridges book
arrived just before Christmas
messages of love caring support

we did not celebrate Christmas
this year
we observed Christmas
day of remembering
happier Christmases
reflection sadness grief

I gave our daughter a photo album
90 8X10s of the two of you
from before her birth until
the last pictures
painful labor of love
dragon mother and child
she will treasure the pictures
over the years
she gave me an acrylic holder
for the fortune
"Love is in the Air"

it was a blue blue Christmas
without you

December 25, 2011 Journal I
transcribed March 21, 2013

Great Circle

life is so fragile so tenuous
if we were fully open
to the fragility of life
we would either be
paralyzed with fright
or incredibly reckless
as it does not appear
to make much difference

I denied the dark side of life
aka death
denied Carol Susan was really ill
knew something was wrong
pretended it was an esoteric
endocrine imbalance
not life threatening
it was much much worse

life and death make no sense
part of the great circle
great circle my ass
fuck the great circle
looks more like an asshole
than anything else

why do old assholes live
compassionate loving people die
old assholes should be struck by lightning
so death could meet its quota
could snap up some young assholes
in the unlikely shortage of old ones

leave the kind loving caring
thoughtful compassionate people alone
at least until they grow well into old age

death appears to have
no facility for discrimination
no moral compass
reaches out randomly
sowing chaos in its wake
chaos and grief

life and death make no sense
part of the great circle
great circle my ass
fuck the great circle
looks more like an asshole
than anything else

December 26, 2011 Journal I
transcribed March 21, 2013

Recovery Higher Purpose

many of the grief books I have read
include a unit on recovery
transforming the loss
moving on
exercises to help
discover the higher purpose of the loss
seem to be promoting
development of rationalizations
divert attention from loss and grief
to recovery transformation
encouraging making up a reason
so people can get on with getting on

a culture of quick recovery
instant gratification
rationalizations
denial
dying taboo
death taboo
grieving taboo
so grieving goes underground
recovery a rationalization away
made up a higher purpose – check
grieving is attenuated
repressed
tears left unshed become frozen
in the hostile environment
the soul weeps
no one listens

without the authentic expression of grief
recovery is pretending
a game played wearing a mask
until the players forget it is a game

of the many dying death grieving books
I have read
Joan Halifax's statement about
honest scouring
seems the most honest
authentic
soulful path
I realize there is little support for honest scouring
so I scour on the installment plan
writing pitiful poems
very slow scouring

I am not going to rationalize
a higher purpose
I am showing compassion for myself
in my need to grieve
I am not going to manufacture a higher purpose
just so I can check grieving off my list
it just ain't that easy
anyone who tells you it is
including the grief books
has a bad case of taboo
which unfortunately is
extremely contagious

December 31, 2011 Journal I
transcribed March 24, 2013

"to scour my heart out with honest sorrow" page 192
Joan Halifax. ***Being with Dying: Cultivating Compassion and Fearlessness in the Presence of Death***. Boston: Shambhala, 2009.

Hellfires of Grief

hellfires of grief
invisible to the naked eye
black fire created by loss
not like ordinary fire

greater the loss
hotter the fire
longer the burning

disembodiment
of my soulmate
creates hottest fire
of all

burning
on and on
burning away impurities
regrets remorse
longing fears
until all that remains
is
love
hellfires of grief
continue
to burn and burn
now and then
I see a touch of gold with silver
around the edges
mostly it is
black
invisible to the naked eye

with more impurities
as the fuel

hellfires of grief
burn
on and on
till
all
that
remains
is
love

I wonder
what that
will look like

1/1/2012 Journal I
transcribed 1/9/2013

Note: My thanks to Marie-Louise Von Franz for her images of "the fire has to burn the fire" page 252 and "setting in hell roasting" page 254
Marie-Louise Von Franz. ***Alchemy: An Introduction to the Symbolism and Psychology***. Toronto: Inner City Books, 1980.

New Years 2012

we cleaned house on Friday
you always started the new year
with a clean house
we honored your tradition
washed bedding and towels
on new year's eve
honoring another of your traditions
we did not honor too many more
not the same without you
here in your physical body

new year's eve
brought the grandfather desk
grandfather chair into the shrine room
near the shrine
next to a picture of you just before
Halloween 1977
holding your first pumpkin
we were both very happy
one of my favorite pictures
one of many wonderful memories
some captured in pictures
all treasured in my heart

I burn incense all day and most of the night
every day
added extra for New Year's Eve
lit candles set at the shrine
talked to you cried
tried to listen

poured a bit of cognac
left half for you and the goddesses
to enjoy the essence
kept one more tradition
held some money at midnight
think money is for prosperity rather than luck
otherwise I have not been holding near enough
the last few years
put money on your urn so you could
share our tradition
know you do not need it
know you like the sharing
remembering our traditions
sending you my love

January 1, 2012 Journal I
transcribed March 21, 2013

Dehydration

after disembodiment of my beloved
intense crying
sobs deep in my chest
painful crying intense crying
trouble breathing
few tears bitter tears burning tears
did not understand
why so few tears
tears soul's blood
bleeding tears

inspiration
knew I was dehydrated
easy to cry
hard to product tears
dehydrated
started drinking water
eight ten twelve
glasses a day
kept a log
after a week more tears
paradoxically felt better to cry
more tears
soul's blood bleeding tears
spilling the tears of grief
strange comfort
bleeding tears

January 2, 2012 Journal I
transcribed March 14, 2013

Despair Golden Dreams

when the spirit of
my most precious other
left her body
what of me remained
only half of what used to be
with the addition of
numbness disbelief
my chest feeling
ripped open
half my heart
gone with her
half left behind
raw bleeding
blood of loss
hellfires of grieving
black night moon
in brightest light of day
dark nights of the soul
nothing prepared me for the impact
cataclysmic
nothing makes sense
anger with no target
anger with little energy
too raw numb
in shock
to realize the full extent
of my loss
energy leaking out with my tears
I discover she is gone
gone
never to return in her physical body

never again to
hold her
see her smile
hear her laughter
smell her fragrance
hear her words
taste her love
intense longing for her physical person
her compassionate ways
her radiant being
her exceptional intellect
her wicked wit
prematurely wise
prematurely gone
gone
never to return in her physical body
intense longing
intense missing
intense grief

desperate to discover the
portal to the subtle spirit realm
too raw
too desperate
too needy
to awaken to the subtle spirit realm

then a golden dream
my beloved appears
subtle spirit form
golden goddess
without needing words
offers her assistance
compassion

love

while I continue to seek
entrance to the subtle spirit realm
when awake
my dreaming body has no difficulty
adjusting to the new form of my beloved
golden dreams
provide far more than words can explain
healing golden dreams
they contain the other half
of my heart

> January 5, 2012 Journal I
> transcribed February 26, 2013

You Miss Her Too Much

I had been shopping for over a year
at the local Asian market
always buying incense and other items
early on Carol Susan went along
then I only wore black and bought a lot more incense
the Asian women asked about Carol Susan
they were sad to hear of her disembodiment
each time they would ask "How long has it been?"
I would answer the number of days
they would tell the women shoppers as I piled
large quantities of incense on the counter
some would nod knowingly – they seemed to know the
hellfires of grief

one day one of the woman ask me
"How long has it been?"
"97 days"
I could see her doing the math in her head
"Asian people only burn incense for 49 days"
"Yes, I know"
"Do you dream of her?"
"Yes, I do"
"You miss her too much.
You burn too much incense.
You are keeping her here."
"Yes I do miss her too much
but I am not burning too much incense
as she is in a wonderful golden place."

I am still burning too much incense
I still miss her too much
I always will

January 7, 2012 Journal II
transcribed October 27, 2012

Special Spoon

Carol Susan and I picked out flatware
all the spoons were oval
except one
one was round
the sugar spoon
I was perplexed when
Carol Susan set the table
I always got the little round spoon
one day I asked her about it
Carol Susan said
it was a "special spoon"
that was why
she gave it to me
after that when ever
I set the table I gave the
special spoon
to my beloved

after Carol Susan disembodied
each time I saw the
little special spoon
I cried held it cried
remembering the tradition
Carol Susan's love

I do not use the little special spoon
any more
I have placed the special spoon
on the shrine
each time I look upon it
I remember feel
Carol Susan's love

January 12, 2012 Journal II
transcribed December 23, 2012

Tiger Balm

I bought Tiger Balm today
if I use the one you bought
eventually it would be gone
I could not handle the loss
so I am saving your Tiger Balm
using the new one

I understand the dynamics of displacement
in my head
my heart does not care
so I am saving your Tiger Balm
using the new one
a small potential loss I can control
I put your Tiger Balm on the shrine
extending compassion to myself
small act of kindness for myself
no blame as the I Ching would say
pleases my heart soul
does no harm

January 13, 2012 Journal II
transcribed March 28, 2013

Lunar New Years Cards

for many years you sent out
Lunar New Years cards
family friends colleagues clients
hundreds of cards from
DeVaney-Wong International
I would help you with the project each year
people collected the cards
put them on display
looked forward to the new ones each
Lunar New Year

this year I continued your tradition
sending our Lunar New Years cards
sent out over two hundred
family friends colleagues clients
pretending I was helping you
once again
told everyone the year of the
black water dragon
would be a sad and dark year for us
mentioned your memorial web site
Taryne Jade created

many people responded
happy to receive another
Lunar New Years card from you
they did not expect to receive any more
Lunar New Years cards
made quite a few cry
made me cry too
pretending I was helping you sending out
Lunar New Years cards again

January 22, 2012 Journal II
transcribed March 28, 2013

Lunar New Year 2012

year of the black water dragon
very appropriate image
black water
black waters of grief
dragon size grief
very appropriate image

I hope to transform the dark image of the
black water dragon
ride on the wings of dragons
to the subtle spirit realm
visit with you

your needing to leave your physical body
will not be as heartbreaking if I can
more frequently visit you
I know I visit you often
golden dreams
problem is my poor memory
for the subtle spirit realm
I only remember a few
wonderful and magnificent
golden dreams

I am hoping for the good fortune
of spiritual prosperity
during the year of the
black water dragon
better memory of
golden dreams

I sipped some cognac at midnight
left the rest for you and White Tara
I hope She does not sniff it all up
She is small but has great power
so I added a little extra
enough for the two of you to share
I held Chinese coins you gave me
placed three Chinese coins on the top of your urn
hoping for spiritual prosperity
for you me our daughter
everyone else

first lunar new year
we have not shared together embodied
in thirty four years
year of the black water dragon
very appropriate image

January 22, 2012 Journal II
transcribed March 28, 2013

Always and Forever

Carol Susan signed cards she gave me
Love Always and Forever
Carol Susan

I often did the same

I have added *beyond*
so now in our journal each entry
to my beloved ends with
I love you
always forever and beyond

always and forever
is enough
I added *beyond* to make sure
there is no doubt regarding my intent

I have seen into beyond
golden dreams
Love Always and Forever Carol Susan
is there

January 30, 2012 Journal II
transcribed March 28, 2013

Soulmates Journey

should you have the supreme good fortune
finding your soulmate in this lifetime
grab on to them
never let them go
do not let anything or anyone
including yourself
prevent you from the experience

merging with your soulmate
soul to soul
heart to heart
mind to mind
body to body
sacred experience
possession in great measure
two become one

the merger of soulmates
experience the sacred spirit realm
in the physical world
creates a golden energy cocoon
the merger sounds both esoteric and easy
the experience is deceptively complex
two as one deposited into
an alchemical crucible
heated by the fires of love
all the rough edges
rubbing together
intimacy of the crucible

requires courage

leaps of faith
open hearts
to enter the crucible
and remain
there are dark times
the crucible generates intense heat
almost unbearablely intense
removing rough edges
allows connections to deepen
become more intense
more intimate
energy flows
soul light shines brighter
not always pretty neat and tidy
crucible can be a frightening place
requires courage
leaps of faith
open hearts
perseverance

if you have the supreme good fortune
of finding you soulmate in this lifetime
grab on to them
never let them go
do not let anything or anyone
including yourself
prevent you from the experience
best experience through all of your lifetimes

should your soulmate
disembody as did mine
you will experience intense despair
the crucible is not gone
more subtle now

perhaps invisible to your eyes
the union continues
soulmates transcend
all barriers
so keep holding on
never let go
requires courage
leaps of faith
wide open hearts
to stay in the crucible
during the darkest times
do not let anything or anyone
including yourself
prevent you from the experience

looking with eyes of love
when eyes of loss
prevail

easy to say

doing

a life's work

February 1, 2012 Journal II
transcribed January 16, 2013

Chakra Energy Connections

when we first met
we formed our golden cocoon
chakras merged as one
blended together synchronized
so many connections
energy filaments everywhere
could not tell them apart
spinning as one
no matter the distance between
our physical bodies
wonderful experiences
energy connections of soulmates
together again
many chakra connections already existed
between us before we met
many life times of connections
we added many new ones
chakras merged as one
within our golden cocoon
our home
across many life times
and beyond

you disembodied
three lower bodies gone
three lower chakras gone
beautiful radiant soul
returned to the spirit realm

thirty four years we shared
our golden cocoon this time
when the lower bodies
lower chakras
disconnected
I experienced them as
torn away
leaving me raw exposed
my chakra cords frayed
flapping about
searching for you
our loving connection
gone
horrible wound
worse experience of my life
at first I could only focus
on the three lower bodies
three lower chakras
gone
intense grief
hellfires of grief
dark nights of the soul
mixed with denial
other defenses

even during the darkest nights
I knew your soul had
separated from your lower bodies
returned to the subtle spirit realm
I could feel your subtle energy presence
your love surrounding me
then wonderful golden dreams
you appear in your radiant golden spirit form

images of lower bodies fading – gone
lower chakras disconnecting – gone
helped to explain the paradox
intense grief
juxtaposed with
golden dreams
you appear as a radiant luminous being
full of compassion and love
two intense experiences

horrible loss of my beloved
my beloved golden spirit visits
both real no matter how
incongruent

I know now our golden cocoon
is not damaged
even though some parts
are missing – transformed
three lower bodies gone
three lower energy centers gone
I will always miss
your three lower bodies
three lower energy centers
your mortal embodiment
I now know the
damage is in my heart
embodied soul
so many connections
so many now damaged
torn from their mates
raw bleeding energy
at first the loss was over powering

too intense to see beyond the grief
psychic pain bleeding energy
then golden dreams
provided an opening to
the subtle spirit realm
I read the golden dreams
again and again
they sooth the charka connections
missing their mates
slow the psychic energy bleeding
provide hope
I carry the golden dreams
in my heart and embodied soul
I remember them always
bring me closer to
the subtle spirit realm
and my beloved

I need to slow down
my lower level chakras seeking
their mates
my lower bodies doing the same
part of my grief work
necessary for healing
the open connections
created by the disembodiment
of my beloved
not easy to stop the search
the golden dreams ease
the frantic nature of the search
slowing down the flailing
helps staunch the ends of the connections
so the loss of energy is less intense
I need the energy to heal

gain access to the subtle spirit realm
my quest to enter the spirit realm
embrace my beloved
awake

I
intend
to

February 19, 2012 Journal II
transcribed March 6-7, 2013

Note: My thanks to Dion Fortune, Barbara Brennan and others for their healing energies and inspirations.

Grief CD

I listened to a grief cd for months
warm friendly voice
talking about grief
I listened to the cd every day
then I got upset about concepts
I started to argue with the voice
told the voice I **did not** feel better
as my denial softened
I experienced more intense grief
I embraced my grief
deep grieving is better
even it feels worse
hellfires of grief

I got angry about the concept
that nothing is lost
my beloved ashes in an urn
at her shrine
perhaps I am too concrete
I lost her physical body
emotional body mental body
no longer in the physical realm

I was too raw dark heavy
to easily embrace the spirit realm
except in our golden dreams
where nothing is lost

I am better at deep grieving
accessing my anger
so the cd had value no blame
I chose not to listen to it anymore

March 16, 2012 Journal III
transcribed January 30, 2013

Widower

awful word awful status
awful demographic
widower sad lonely word
sad lonely reality
nothing worse
becoming a widower
world irrevocably changed
hellfires of grief
lost without my companion's
physical body
not a culture to mourn
overt grief expressions taboo
widower sneaks off
nurse my wounds in private
bleed words of grief onto our journal
write poems in dark of night
for spirit eyes to read
we cry together sharing our loss
deepest wound
holding on by a thread
wondering why
physical companion gone
our world in chaos
hellfires of grief

external world adjusts easily
new demographic status
bank removes your name
credit union freezes our account
DMV refuses to issue new tags on line
widower must show up titles in hand

remove your name from titles
car insurance eliminated your name
changed my status to widower
home owners insurance too
signed tax returns as surviving spouse
each event another harsh encounter
reality of my demographic status
widower
next year for tax purposes I will
be considered single

I know my legal status
awful demographic widower
most every institution
local state federal governments
processed your death certificate instantly
changed both our statuses
made it harder to pretend
I would take a little time
for the reality to sink in
forced into the widower's box instantly

my heart and soul knows
another reality
my heart of hearts knows
our love transcends
physical limits
I visit you in our shared golden dreams
I am not a widower in the spirit realm
we are together
always forever and beyond

March 21, 2012 Journal III
transcribed April 8, 2013

Grief Work

I told my grief counselor

that at a day for a day

a week for a week

a month for a month

a year for a year

I would be 102 before

my grief work would be finished

she did not think I was joking

she knew my language was of the heart

the heart measures by intensity

not by calendar or clock

and should I reach 102

would my grief work really be done

of course not

March 20, 2012 Journal III
transcribed November 22, 2012

Disembodiment

I use the word
disembodiment
rather than the word
death
as we are embodied
when our
souls enter our bodies
disembodied when our souls leave

death even *death-to-the-body*
is not as fully true as
disembodiment

the soul speaks of disembodiment
rather than death
since the soul relocates

to those left behind the pain of loss
is not lessened by the terms we use

disembodiment
says we know our loved ones
are just behind the veil

we miss their physical person
grieve the loss of their physical person
but we know our loved ones
are just behind the veil
knowing provides a
measure of comfort

March 27, 2012 Journal III
transcribed November 27, 2012

Only those who take leisurely what the people of the world are busy about
can be busy about what the people of the world take leisurely.
                                                             Chuang Tzu

Priorities

quote posted on our desk for many years
looked at it often
talked about it
tried to follow the wisdom
often failed
wasted time squandered time
doing stupid things
projects work chores reading
could have lived a simpler life
enjoyed more time together
too late now
except for
regrets remorse sorrow
talked about balance
often did not follow my advice

since your disembodiment
I invent projects chores
so I do not cry all the time
temporary diversions
distractions
grief too intense
too much of a bad thing
so I create distractions
no blame
compassion
grief finds me

anyway
catches up
makes up for lost time

I know the projects chores
are mostly meaningless
temporary diversions
from the hellfires of grief
a few may help with healing
projects chores I take leisurely
busy with the experience of grief
not concerned with balance
it can look after itself
grieving is the path with heart
soul's work of healing
painful way to learn
priorities

March 22, 2012 Journal III
transcribed February 5, 2013

Note: My thanks to Chuang Tzu for words of wisdom and inspiration.
quote from:
Lin Yutang. *The Importance of Living*. New York: Harper, 1937/1965/1996. (page 323)

Old People Couples

I get distressed seeing old people
physically alive
you are not

I get distressed seeing couples
physically together
we are not

I get more distressed seeing old couples
physically growing old together
we are not

I do not envy them
what they have
makes me sad
reminds me of what
we had and lost

I do not want to trade
places with any of them

I just want you back
then I would not be distressed
ever again
I promise

March 24, 2012 Journal III
transcribed January 29, 2013

New Restaurant

went to lunch at a new Chinese restaurant

hostess set me at a small table with one chair

she started to leave changed her mind

told me I would be more comfortable in a booth

she knew I needed room for your spirit

she also knew you prefer a booth

she has gifts she may not fully realize

she realized we were there together

we have always tried out new places together

this was no exception

March 29, 2012 Journal III
transcribed January 29, 2013

Three Great Events

three great events of my life

waking up to mythology
ever expanding realms of reality
language of souls
spirit realm

merging with my soulmate
intimacy of souls
souls love song
possession in great measure

disembodiment of my soulmate
hellfires of grief – dark nights of the soul
spirit realm where half my heart and soul reside
possession in great measure

I thought I understood something of the I Ching
now I know better
I do know a little about Hexagram 14
possession in great measure

April 2, 2012 Journal III
transcribed January 27, 2013

Home

you are always home for me
we are home when we are together
no matter where we are
I know you feel the same

since you disembodied
finding my way home
is more of a challenge
the spirit realm
is home now

home has always been where ever you are
you are always home for me
we are home when we are together
no matter where we are
I know you feel the same

April 4, 2012 Journal III
transcribed January 29, 2013

Easter 2012

you loved for us to get dressed up
go to a fancy Easter brunch
every year we decorated the house
colored eggs
giant colored eggs outside
you were always the Easter Bunny
put special treats in our baskets
late at night
now Easter is just another sad holiday
special only in memories
stored in our hearts
you were always the Easter Bunny
in your physical body
spirit of the holiday left with you
you were the spirit of the holiday
center of our family
holidays will never be the same

our holiday decorations are stored in boxes
sound asleep in the garage
I do not think they will ever wake up
I do not know what to do with them
so I let them sleep
I wonder if they dream of holidays gone by
memories of happy times
when you were here
in your physical body
spirit of the holidays
center of the family
I wonder if the decorations can sense the

darkness surrounding holidays now
sense your subtle energy presence
I know your subtle presence
remembers holidays
sad you are not here
in your physical body
to restore them to their former joy
I do not know if the decorations can
sense your subtle energy presence
I can

April 8, 2012 Journal III
transcribed March 27, 2013

Materialize–Catching Up

all the grief work in the world
will not bring you back
I cannot explain why I believe it should
I am left in this realm with
memories photographs things
mostly sadness and regret
worse experience of my life

everything seems so silly and stupid now
career ambition projects reading
I wasted time I could have spent with you
most of all I wish you were still here
in your physical body without the cancer
that is all I really want
cannot have

I am raw and suffering
from your disembodiment
while I know it is not rational
somehow I expect to see you
for you to appear
in your physical body
I hope to see you
become disappointed
over and over
when you do not appear
then I cry and feel stupid
for holding out such hope

I do not fully accept that your physical person
is gone even though I know it has
your ashes are in your urn at the shrine
makes no difference to my heart
I keep hoping your body will materialize
I will be able to hold you once again
then I become discouraged and cry

I visit you in the spirit realm
in our golden dreams
I know our union has only changed forms
sounds easy in theory is difficult in practice
since my spirit eyes and ears are in development
you are already there ahead of me
waiting for me to catch up
as usual

you naturally understand the mysteries
while I read study try to learn with my head
what you know instinctively
I need to catch up
I will sooner or later

April 13, 2012 Journal III
transcribed January 30, 2013

Get On With It

our culture does not
deal well with
death
grief
morning
makes people
uncomfortable
even afraid
angry to be reminded
the cold hand of death
will one day touch
the ones they love
the most

so I do
"get on with it"
grieving
morning
experiencing
hellfires of grief
dark nights of the soul
my reality
my truth
my path with heart
anything else would be
living a lie

April 15, 2012 Journal III
transcribed January 29, 2013

Heart Break

I do not know how
my heart can keep breaking
over and over
still have anything
left to break
but it does
over and over and over
several times in minutes

the first break
was half in two
leaving only
half behind

the other half
went with you
to the
spirit realm

I do not know how
my heart can keep breaking
over and over
but it does

April 22, 2012 Journal III
transcribed January 29, 2013

Six Months

today six month observance
of your disembodiment
when you beautiful radiant spirit
vacated your physical body
observance not celebration
thankful you are free from
your physical body's pain
heart breaking to see you suffer
though you were so very graceful
six months ago today
anticipatory grief became
hellfires of grief
burning and burning
dark nights of the soul

dusted tidied your shrine
cleaned house yard a few days before
our cottage tidy for the observation
six months
worse experience of my life
placed a new purple orchid at your shrine
many blooms buds to open
as your birthday approaches
planted two red roses
where we used to sit in the yard
between the miniature fruit trees
planted thirteen white irises
named immortality
why I got them
made me cry

dark purple almost black iris
I planted in the fall almost open
be fully open for your birthday
sad you will not see it with your physical eyes
I read the cards and notes
you gave me over the years
I saved them all each and every one
you saved the ones I gave you too
keep them in drawers at the shrine
read them with tears in my eyes
golden feeling in my heart of hearts
I know your presence surrounds me
I feel your golden love
sometimes only faintly
since I am dark heavy with the
hellfires of grief
dark nights of the soul
six months since your disembodiment
worse experience of my life

six months
I miss your physical person
grateful for your spirit presence
golden dreams
six months
dark nights of the soul
hellfires of grief
burning and burning
worse six months of my life

April 29, 2012 Journal III
transcribed March 30, 2013

Carol Susan's Birthday 2012

today is your birthday
the day your physical body was born
fifty-eight years ago
if you were still embodied
started celebrating your birthdays
together in 1977
your last two embodied birthdays
fifty-six fifty-seven
you had chemo days before them both
awful birthday presents
we still celebrated
you had such courage
grace elegance
even though your body was
traumatized poisoned
cancer surgery chemo
you said very little about the pain
I do not understand how you managed
to be so
graceful appreciative
heart centered even then
sad loving memories
remembering your birthdays

would take too many words to describe
your fifth-eighth birthday
first since you disembodied
we honored your birthday
celebrating your life
as best as we know how

remembering
put purple irises around the cottage
Chinese food for lunch
your favorites
burned extra incense
planted two purple passion vines
more rose bushes
I sit at the shrine
remembering your birthdays
other things
crying wishing you were
still here in your physical body
sipped a bit of cognac
left the rest for you
and the Goddesses
celebrated as best we knew how
I know you were present for your birthday
remembering with us
your birthday always a day of celebration
grateful we are together
in whatever form
sharing birthdays together

May 8, 2012 Journal III
transcribed March 29, 2013

National Shrine Visit 2012

pilgrimage to the National Shrine
few days after your birthday
never there without your physical person
went to the lower level to visit
Mary, Mother of Mankind
your favorite statue of
Mother Mary at the Shrine
you would visit Her
when you were in college
living next door
one of your favorite places
I lit candles set there softly crying
remembering all the times we went
to the shrine lit candles together
thirty four years of visits together
not enough
I wanted a small statue of
Mary, Mother of Mankind
to put at your shrine
not available got a picture of Her
small abstract statue of Mother Mary
add to Kuan Yin and White Tara
sister Goddesses at your shrine
discovered Mary, Mother of Humankind
was dedicated May 8, 1938
on your birthday few years apart
sad to be at the National Shrine
without your physical person
good to light candles

many candles
I could feel your presence
as we lit candles together
you hand on mine
both remembering other
happier times
both embodied
there together

May 12, 2012 Journal III
transcribed March 29, 2013

Mother's Day 2012

first Mother's Day without
the physical person of
my mothering one
before you were a biological mother
you were my mothering one
before our daughter was born
we celebrated Mothering One's Day
some may not have understood
you were my mothering one
after our daughter was born
we celebrated
Mother's Day Mothering One's Day
combined
two little ones
one full time
one now and then
I was your mothering one
though not exceptional as you
good enough with moments of
exceptionality
you were exceptional almost all the time
Dragon Mother
Dragon Mothering One
very best kind

others treasured your nurturing ways
we got the lion's share
you always had more than enough
spoiled by your exceptional mothering
made Mother Day

Mothering One's Day
exceptionally painful
spent most of the day remembering
your exceptional mothering ways
spoiled rotten by your
exceptional mothering
grateful for the years
heartbroken by the disembodiment
of my exceptional mothering one
I miss my mothering one too much
I always will

know you are still my mothering one
different form
subtle spirit mothering one
exceptional mothering one
always forever and beyond

May 13, 2012 Journal IV
transcribed April 2, 2013

34th Wedding Anniversary

our wedding happiest day of my life
we shared our connection
beyond our physical embodiment
wedding of soulmates spiritmates
always forever and beyond

universe in perfect alignment
you were so beautiful radiant
both beyond happy
joined together in our golden cocoon

34th wedding anniversary
first since you disembodied
black painful day
remembering
sad day for you
remembering
sharing our lives
side by side
together

we are still together making new memories
different form
beyond physical embodiment
visit in our golden dreams
wedding of soulmates spiritmates
always forever and beyond

July 30, 2012 Journal V
transcribed April 4, 2013

Nine Months

one day after our 34th wedding anniversary
memories of
golden love light energy
nine months since your disembodiment
memories filled with
black pain tears longing
hellfires of grief
dark night of the soul

I miss your physical person
so lonely without my companion
in your physical body
no matter where I am
not the same
you were always so happy to see me
your loving smile nourished me
when nothing else could
you have always been
the most important person
to me

before each black dark date
I become sadder grieve
experience ever hotter
hellfires of grief
blacker dark nights of the soul

memories golden dreams
keep me from being swallowed up by
the dark nights
burned up by the hellfires of grief
memories golden dreams with you

July 31, 2013 Journal V
transcribed April 4, 2013

First I Ching Together

consulting the I Ching
I found your first hexagrams
you consulted the I Ching
March 3, 1977
first use of the I Ching together
we both know the question

changing lines
first hexagram 38: opposition
image of flames above lake below
flames burn upward
lake seeps downward
movements in opposition
not a good beginning
but a good end

we had much opposition at the start
effected a good end superior beginning

second hexagram 14: possession in great measure
image of flame above heaven below
fire in heaven above
possession in great measure
supreme success

finding our soulmate again
love of soulmates
merging and sharing
possession in great measure
supreme success

possession in great measure
has a dark side
hellfires of grief
dark nights of the soul
I am working to effect a good end
to the hellfires of grief
dark nights of the soul
I see it now and then
our shared golden dreams
possession in great measure
in the spirit realm
our union continues
different form
more subtle
possession in great measure
soulmates
spiritmates
spirit realm
possession in great measure

July 31, 2012 Journal V
transcribed February 15, 2013

Reference:
Richard Wilhelm (translation) Cary F Baynes (English translation). **The I Ching or Book of Changes, Volume I**. London: Routledge and Kegan Paul, Ltd., 1951.

Soul Lessons

according to sources
this realm is a school
we sign up for lessons
so we can learn
new experiences
agreed to before hand
to endure horrible pain
suffering loss grief
heartbreak despair
damn if I remember
signing up
for anything like this
must not have read
the fine print
too late to renegotiate
hard assed school
no compassion I comprehend
if I could comprehend
might not need the lesson
sure there are more lessons
waiting
this lesson is more than
enough for me

August 13, 2012 Journal V
transcribed April 7, 2013

New Circumstances

I send you all my love
all my energy
to comfort you
help you adjust to your
new circumstances
not easy leaving
loved ones behind
when you go ahead
so I am sending you
all my love
all my energy
I know you like
my sending you
all my love
all my energy
even if you do not need it
you are glad to know
I am sending
all my love
all my energy
anyway

August 13, 2012 Journal V
transcribed April 7, 2013

My Birthday 2012

you always made each event special
birthdays anniversaries holidays
all celebrations
each one was memorable
magic ingredient your love
since your disembodiment
not much for celebrations
observations through my tears
first birthday without you here
in your physical body
for 34 years
worse birthday of my life

until you became ill
I did not feel my
chronological age
black cloud depleted my energy
aged ten years almost over night

what I want for my birthday
you here again in your
physical body healthy
my head knows will not happen
you would be here already if
hoping wishing longing
made it so
miss your "old coat"
your golden chrysalis
understand metamorphosis
intellectually
not pretty up close

nor simple

have trouble seeing the butterfly
feel the butterfly's presence
the butterfly feels more like
a golden rainbow dragon
to me
experience the
golden rainbow dragon
in my dreams
best birthday present

better still
golden dreams
not just for birthdays
golden dreams happen
all the time
I only remember
some of them
it is enough
for now

August 20, 2012 Journal VI
transcribed April 7, 2013

GIFTS

I gave you a necklace of seven bright tiny stars
strung with the gold and silver cords of my love
in the middle was the ruby star of my love

I gave you a song
only you and I can hear

you said thank you and smiled warmly
you know they had been yours all along
Always Forever and Beyond

you gave me precious gifts
you gave me joy
happiness
love
moon sun stars
rainbows from Our Mother

you gave me a song
only you and I can hear

we share our golden cocoon
we share our souls
we share the pain of our separation
each in their own way
your disembodiment is the hardest lesson
I continue to look for you and cry

September 20, 2012 Journal VI
transcribed November 20, 2012

Enough

I miss you "too much"
I do not know how much
"too much" might be
but I miss you way way way more
than "too much"
sorting sadness grief from suffering
real loss more than enough
do not need to embellish with suffering
nor do I need to turn grief into a virtue
access the subtle spirit realm grieve less
free up the energy used to
fuel the hellfires of grief
so I can visit with you more
in the subtle spirit realm
then I would not need to grieve as much
I do miss your physical person "too much"
what we experienced together
when we were both embodied
many years of treasured memories
of you our love life together
just not enough since it ended
thought occurred to me
spirit realm timeless eternal forever
forever might be enough
not by much
forever will be enough
to be on the safe side I will add
always forever and beyond
that will be enough

September 30, 2012 Journal VII
transcribed April 13, 2013

Shining Moment

our shining is for much more than a moment
we were golden together in our golden cocoon
glowing like a very bright moon
with the black gold light of our Mother
which sometimes turned red white
rainbow colors
I remember all those times
I miss the physical closeness
rainbow bodies together in our golden cocoon
the fireworks the heat of the sun
the cool light of the moon
our connection in the spirit realm is vastly superior
we knew that level in this physical realm
that is where the shining energy and voltage comes from

then we took on dark aspects
awful dark aspects
yet the shining was always there
your beautiful and radiant soul
trapped inside your worn out physical body
always shining
your golden love never faltered
even during the worst of times
you maintained a beautiful grace

our shining continues in a different form
golden and black golden dreams
still shining with energy and voltage
our shining is for much more than a moment
unless that moment is infinity

October 4, 2012 Journal VII
transcribed December 1, 2012

Reference: Robert Bly and Marion Woodman. ***Maiden King: The Reunion of Masculine and Feminine.*** New York: Henry Holt and Company, 1998.

Beyond

beyond sensations
beyond feelings
beyond thoughts
beyond words
to images
beyond images
beyond polarity
to heart, soul, spirit
into the mysteries

the wise person does not
attempt to name the mysteries
with words or images
like trying to encounter the totality of a
giant sequoia whose roots
are hidden
you can see only one section at a time
as you move around the giant
to take in a new part
the other parts are only memories
or totally hidden
nor do you see the seasonal changes
nor the growth from a tiny seed

if you are very quiet extend your soul
with respectful intent
you may touch the soul of the tree.
if it is willing

it is only one tree

these are only words

October 13, 2012

Written on the occasion of reading *The Soul Is Here For Its Own Joy: Sacred Poems from Many Cultures.* edited by Robert Bly, New York: HarperCollins, 1995.

Negative Thoughts

raw dark heavy with grief

missing your physical person

blinds me to the subtle realm of spirit

trying too hard

does not help either

believing the way

is difficult is a

limiting self-fulfilling prophesy

negative thoughts attract

negative energy

positive thoughts attract

positive energy

amazingly simple

powerfully true

October 14, 2012 Journal VII
transcribed December 3, 2012

Clean Towels Double Sinks

I washed towels
transferred Carol Susan's
hand towel and wash cloth
from her side to mine
so she would have new fresh ones

made me cry

I said
"your spirit body does not need towels
I wish with all my heart
you were here to use towels
use toilet paper like no tomorrow
there have been no tomorrows
for 11 months and 15 days
your spirit body
does not need toilet paper
either"

made me cry

I put fresh towels on Carol Susan's
side of the double sink
I still miss you too much
I always will

October 15, 2012

A Dragon Named Grief: Year One

a year ago I started riding the tail of
a dragon named grief

the dragon named grief took up residence in my
heart
sometimes leaked from my eyes
constricted my throat so I could hardly talk
even moan
filled my mind with images memories raged
sweet then bitter

for a long while I rode on the tail being
whipped around without
even the illusion of control
then I moved up front behind the head tried to
steer the beast
with no success

so I jumped into the dragon's mouth to be
consumed – eaten alive
hoping to eventually be born from the dragon
still smelling of the dragon named grief
a child of the dragon named grief
a newborn in an old body

the dragon named grief spread
dropped into my center
area awoke to the hellfires of grief
the pain of loss

I'm still in the body of the dragon named grief
the dragon named grief is still in my body

the dragon named grief and I will be together a long time
we are not friends but we are learning to coexist most of the time
I have learned that the hellfires of grief are the hottest fires of all
the dragon named grief the quickest path to the dark nights of the soul
there are no maps to the exit and no signs
the dragon named grief has a very long digestive tract

now and then I visit the golden spirit realm
leaving the dragon named grief behind
for a little while

October 31, 2012

Black Mola Dress

your black mola dress hung in the shrine room
in our cottage
it was one of the last things you wore
on your physical body
I never washed it
I hung it in front of our closet - on your side
I looked at it every day and held it close to me cried
it was one of the last things you wore
on your physical body

they took your black and gold dragon robe
when they took
your soul-less-spirit-less physical body
they never gave it back
so your black mola dress was the last thing
you wore on your physical body
I had to hold on to

the shrine room has many things of yours
four windows
when we moved I brought some of the shrine
your black mola dress
the shrine is in the bedroom
your black mola dress
was hung in the center of the closet
with my black robe
looked as if I was holding you-embracing you- I was
I stood with your black mola dress held it cried
I put my head on the dress kissed the dress
talked to you about loss
missing

         sadness
          pain
but most of all about loving you

    then I became uneasy about the closet
          I did not like it after dark
         it gave me goose-bumps all over
closet had over three months of accumulated grief
  like a thick dark cloud – trapped and very intense
       so I purged the closet of the grief energy
            the closet felt some better

    something was still unhappy in the closet
        it was our mola bag with the twin owls
    holding our early papers did not like the closet
              I purged the closet again
  put the twin owl mola bag our papers on the shrine
       the twin owl mola bag and papers are
              happy to be at the shrine

         on November 2 – All Souls Day
        I realized the image of my robe holding
           your black mola dress a metaphor
                for my holding on to
       the last fragments of your physical body
         a year after your disembodiment
              I was holding on to the
         faintest aspect of your physical person
        you were ready for me to let go
              I cried and cried because
  the black mola dress was the last thing you wore
              on your physical body
                I had to hold on to
     I had held on with all my will and intent

my chakra cords connected
to the faintest whispers of your physical presence
you let me
because you love me
you were ready for me to let you go

so I held the black mola dress one last time
kissed it
I needed the small comfort of your faintest physical
presence
for the first year
it was a gift of your love
I was releasing you because of my love for you
I folded the black mola dress held it to my heart
it was the last thing you wore
on your physical body
I had to hold on to
as an act of love I knew I did not
have to hold on to it any more
I disconnected the chakra cords
the last fragments of
your physical presence were free to go
I took the black mola dress folded to the shrine
placed it under the double owl mola bag

later that night I found that something
was still wrong with the closet
I knew your physical presence
was free and gone
I went into the closet to determine
what was wrong
on the floor in front of the space
where your black mola dress
had been with my black robe were

my foot prints in the carpet
as it was 4am I decided to vacuum in the morning
I purged the area as best as I could
of the residual energy in the footprints
but knew a through vacuuming would be needed
so I contained the energy for the rest of the night
vacuumed the carpet severely in the morning

now your black mola dress is folded and empty
of the last of your physical energy
your black mola dress is still the last thing I have
that you wore on your physical body
I am no longer holding on to your black mola dress
or holding on to your faint physical presence

I have cried and cried and know I did the right thing
the path of heart and soul
right action-right heart-right mind

now the closet is only just a closet
your black mola dress is neatly folded at the shrine
filled with memories and love
nothing more – nothing less
in a place of honor – a sacred place
at the shrine and in my heart
Always
Forever
And
Beyond

later thinking about the very hard day
I thanked you for your gift of the year
you knew I needed the comfort
provided by even the smallest amount
of your physical presence
I knew it was time for me to let you go
you whispered "Thank you little bunny."
I said "You are welcome. I love you."

November 2, 2012

Forgiveness

complaining about my lack of progress
in my quest to access the spirit realm
Carol Susan's voice
"a lot of it has to do with forgiveness"
inspirational message
my beloved's helping from the other side
perhaps I have not fully forgiven myself
for squandering time
straying from the soul's way
taking time for granted
assuming we had many more years
embodied together
too much time energy working projects
being a flawed human being
I wonder how total self forgiveness
needs to be to be effective
perfection in forgiveness
one hundred percent
what is enough forgiveness
I do not know
I have sort of forgiven myself
I wonder if that is enough
my quest requires
patience perseverance compassion
compassion includes forgiveness
I am working on it

October 29, 2012 Journal VII
transcribed April 13, 2013

Assimilating the Dragon

swallowed by the dragon named grief
perceiving the dragon as separate
much larger than me
swallowed by a giant alien
know the grief dragon is part of me
most of me
rest small balled up thing
in the dragon's stomach
eaten alive by the dragon named grief

now I am eating the grief dragon
from the inside out
huge grief dragon
grief food awful meal
grief dragon worst tasting
hard to chew harder to swallow
bitter sour nasty tasting
assimilating the dragon named grief
slow painful process
work of grief
recovering the grief dragon's energy
my energy the dragon consumed
eating the dragon who ate me
recovering my energy

while I am assimilating the grief dragon
the grief dragon is transforming me
fueled by grief dragon
distributed throughout my person
I need the converted energy
of the grief dragon

to embrace the spirit realm
so the dragon meat of grief
is mine
I will assimilate every bite
no matter how long it takes

eating grief dragon
has effects
I do not recommend looking
at me sideways
every part of me is infused
with grief dragon
you might catch a glimpse
of the grief dragon's shadow
transformed and assimilated
into every cell
grief dragon's shadow
never goes away
so I am eating the grief dragon
who ate me
ugly messy painful grief work
assimilating the grief dragon
recovering the grief dragon's energy
my energy the dragon consumed
eating the dragon who ate me
recovering my energy
bite by nasty awful painful bite

November 11, 2011 Journal IIX
transcribed April 9, 2013

Life Review

books tell about people
who pass over to the other side
the spirit realm
experience a past life review
I do not remember from
other times
so I do not know
I know for the past year
I have been experiencing
my own life review
before I pass over
to the spirit realm

I have remembered all
my fumbling ways
squandering time
errors of omission
errors of commission
the hellfires of grief
not a forgiving
or compassionate
location for a life review
dark heavy harsh
glaring look back

not all darkness
I can remember the golden times
intense love companionship
intimacy sharing of
soulmates spiritmates

under all the grief loss sadness
tarnish of life's experiences
we have always been
golden rainbow dragons together
always forever and beyond

my life review continues
even in the hellfires of grief
I am gaining improved
perspective balance
my visits to the spirit realm
in golden dreams with you
suggests my life to be
much bigger and better
more complex multidimensional
than I ever imagined

now I am not sure my review
of my past life is always the past
sometimes it seems like the future
sometimes the past
sometimes time seems irrelevant
no time at all
timelessness
golden dreams
immense power energy love
thankful we share them together
transformed my life review
recognize two golden rainbow dragons
residing in the spirit realm
always forever and beyond

November 12, 2012 Journal IIX
transcribed April 9, 2013

"Dead Woman Walking" Pancreatic Cancer

pancreatic cancer action network color is purple
energy field around pancreatic cancer is **black**

when Carol Susan got the diagnosis of
pancreatic cancer
medical community's response was "I'm sorry"

when Carol Susan talked to attorneys about the
two years of progressive symptoms
without a diagnosis appropriate diagnostic
testing or treatment response was it
"does not matter anyway
since the outcome is the same"

which is inaccurate but "conventional wisdom"

Carol Susan said she was treated like a
"dead woman walking"

changing the energy field from black to purple
means changing "conventional wisdom"

survival rate remaining unchanged
for the last 40 years is black

earlier diagnosed and treated
better the rate of survival

most reach stage IV before discovery

Carol Susan survived for almost two years
post diagnosis and surgery

I wish the energy field around
pancreatic cancer was purple
color of hope

energy field around pancreatic cancer is **black**

November 22, 2012

Note: Written on the occasion of reading PanCan's annual report.

Carnival Rides of Grief

on the sooner or later
we all have
multiple turns
on the
carnival rides of grief

where the rides are not rated
the admission price
much too high

first death gives you the ticket
but it is far from free

then death takes the ticket
the ride does not stop
but goes on and on

sooner or later
we all have
multiple turns
on the
carnival rides of grief

November 23, 2012

Holidays Are Hell

holidays are hard
holidays are hell
holiday music
holiday decorations
holiday celebrations

Halloween starts after the 4th of July
Thanksgiving starts before Halloween
Christmas starts before Thanksgiving
holidays are hell

sometimes people who seem festive
irritate me
then I remind myself I had that once myself
silently wish them a happy holiday
try to forgive myself for such small thinking

mostly holidays make me sad
remembering what used to be
is no longer

yes holidays are hell
anniversaries birthdays
disembodiment days

yes holidays anniversaries birthdays
disembodiment days are hell
the other days are not much better
yes loss and grief are hell

November 23, 2012

Paradox of Love

I pour out all

of my love

to you

and yet

my heart

is always

full of

love for you

November 26, 2012

Soul Food

love

is

the

food

of

the

soul

November 26, 2012

Masters Naturally

we invited
two Taoist masters
two Zen masters
two Jedi masters
two Yoga masters
to come stay with us
they are always fully present
one of our special helpers
said they are healers too
their names are
Maya and Merlin
Maya is sable
Merlin is champagne
they are brother and sister
they are Burmese kittens

they are not the least bit worried
about the lofty expectations
we have for them
it is all natural for them
humans are the ones who
have to relearn everything

November 28, 2012

Quest

I

strive

to

become

more

aware

of

our

subtle

spirit

embrace

November 30, 2012

too subtle

sorry I wrote in our journal
too raw too dark too heavy
too whatever
to properly encounter
the spirit realm
that it is too subtle for me
I do not know how many times
I have written that
too many for you
even too many for me
that the subtle spirit realm is
too subtle for me
except for our shared
golden dreams
my quest is to not need to
write it is too subtle for me
ever again
I will persevere until that is true
or until it is no longer necessary
whichever comes first

November 29, 2012 Journal IIX
transcribed April 10, 2013

Surrounding Grief

surrounding
grief
and
sadness
is
my
love

your
love
is
all
around
and
inside
holding
me
in
a
subtle
embrace

November 30, 2012

Eyes of Love Eyes of Loss

during a difficult time
nothing compared to now
Carol Susan gave me
a sticky note that said
"you cannot direct the wind
but you can adjust the sails"
I saved it look at it
from time to time
I understand much better
with a broken heart
year plus of the
hellfires of grief
dark nights of the soul

now I know
I can look from the eyes of love
and
I can look from the eyes of loss

looking through the eyes of love I see
sweet memories abundance
many blessings good fortune
possession in great measure

looking through the eyes of loss I see
sweet memories turn bitter
deprivation sadness
loneliness misfortune
grief in great measure

it is not either or
my small self peers from the mind's eye of loss
my soul sees with the eyes of the heart

my soul knows that the union with my beloved
has only changed forms
my small self focuses on the loss of my beloved's
physical person

my small self fumbles with the sails
my soul is an expert
showing the way

I know that I will always
have the eyes of loss
for the loss is real

I intend to take the path with heart
look mostly from the eyes of love

December 6, 2012

Grounding First

looking at your picture
I have such longing
I think
if I could pierce the veil
access the portal to the other side
I might be sorely tempted
to just float away
so I need to keep
working on grounding
sending my roots deep into Mother Earth
before I access the other side awake
perhaps that is why I am not
having more success
the Universe is conspiring to help me
honor my promise
I am glad in a paradoxical way
my mind is impatient and selfish
my soul knows the path with heart
my soul knows without deep roots
while the branches reach to heaven
the tree may be blown away
by the first strong storm
the Universe is conspiring to help me
honor my promise
I am glad in a paradoxical way

December 2, 2012

Ten Thousand Things

our golden cocoon

is one of the

ten

thousand

things

we are there

together

and

before

December 6, 2012

Holiday Season

bumping up against the holidays
I feel more discouraged
buying crap when I would rather
not celebrate Christmas
any holiday
no holiday festiveness
not inflict my mood
nor pretend otherwise

thankful we shared many holidays
when you were embodied
want to share holidays more fully
with your spirit form
best present
saving the reanimation of your
physical form pre-disease
which I suspect is unlikely

feeling sad lonely heavy dark raw
seeing with eyes of loss
holiday season turns up the heat
hellfires of grief seem hotter
challenge to be spirit warrior
when courage and intent
bump up against the holidays

December 10, 2012 Journal IIX
transcribed April 11, 2013

Invisible Earthquake

grief is not like an earthquake
no visible signs of injured dead
no devastation no tsunamis
no numbers on the Richter scale
no waiting for aftershocks

the loss of one's beloved
invisible earthquake inside
heart broken tears longing
regrets sadness loneliness
outside the world looks the same
the personal world is devastated
by the cataclysmic event
that does not have a number and
aftershocks that go on and on

other loved ones experience
the loss in their own way
each has their own
invisible earthquake of the heart and
aftershocks that go on and on

outside the world looks the same
inside the world has changed
forever

grief is not like an earthquake
unless you look inside

December 11, 2012

Abandonment

to my small self your disembodiment
feels like abandonment

my soul knows this is not true

my small self believes if I had only done better
you would have not gone away

my soul knows this is not true

my small self feels Kali's ways are
mean cruel wasteful

my soul knows it is not that simple

when your soul rejected your physical body
my small self took it personally

my soul knows
my small self's belief is incorrect

my small self struggles to
find the path with heart

my soul knows this is true

my small self tries to
understand access the subtle realm

my soul knows this is true

my small self perseveres
trying to hear the
whispering of his soul
and
his beloveds

both souls know this is true
are glad

my small self wants to solve
see beyond the mysteries

my soul gazes
into the mysteries
in
awe

December 13, 2012

Little Creature

my little self
does not understand
the absence of his
mothering one
the loss of your
loving nurturance

the little creature
waits for you
to return
with tears streaming
from his eyes
gaping hole in
his heart

the little creature
is lost with out
his mothering one
curled up in the corner
whimpering
waiting
for you to return

I am not very good
at being the mothering one
to the little creature
with my focus on
metaphysics
seeking
the path with heart
the subtle energy realm

so the little creature
has been twice abandoned
lost
alone
devastated

through the eyes of the
little creature
abandonment is real
death-to-the-body
not understood
disembodiment
too complex a concept
for the little creature
to comprehend

the little creature
waits for you to come home
spoil me some more

December 13, 2012

Mothering the Little Child

recovery of the
little child
out of my head
into the heart
of the child
looking from the
eyes of the
child
who has lost
his mothering one
ignored
by the
questing
searching
one
who will need
to figure out
how to mother
the little child
as best I can

December 13, 2012

Grief Spiral

my little self
has come out
from being
in shock
now looking
for his
mothering one
as the
spiral of grief
drops lower
expands
to include
more aspects
of
my
totality

December 16, 2012

your little creature awakening

your little creature is waking up
curled up in a ball for over 400 days
with your disembodiment
he went into shock
refused to open his eyes
knows you whisper to him
all the time
can faintly hear you
knows your love is around him
filling his little creature heart
very painful time to be awakening
any time would be
so this time no better or worse
another level of grief work
another turn of the spiral of grief

little creature can see the subtle realm
may not know it to be a separate reality
mostly he wants his mothering one
to hold him tightly to you again
perhaps he slept through some of the
golden dreams
I will read them to him now
he seems to be awakening
guess he needed the protection of
being in a state of shock
defenses in the service of the ego
allows functioning on automatic pilot
withdraw a little at a time

let out a little grief wrapped around
a memory image feeling or two
installment plan grieving

perhaps the little creature can help
with the quest to the spirit realm
little creature can see the subtle spirit realm
may not know it to be a separate reality
mostly he wants his mothering one
to hold him tightly to you again
perhaps he slept through the golden dreams
I will read them to him now he
seems to be awakening
guess he needed the protection of
being in a state of shock
he is not the only one

December 15, 2012 Journal IIX
transcribed April 12, 2013

Night Journey

sky path is not the way
to access the spirit realm
yang way seeks the light
does not look into the shadows

dark path moon light path
underground way
to the heart of
our
Mother
yin way to embrace
spirit realm

mind does not
know the way
nor can the way
be explained

heart and soul
access the spirit realm
with ease assisted by
Goddesses of Compassion

I will need to
embrace the
complex compassion of
Kali
to fully embrace
spirit realm
to hear the spirit voice
of my beloved

I do not like
or understand
Kali
but I must
approach Her
to receive the
dark wisdom
of Her
complex compassion
approach must
be of the heart and soul
respectful
yet with courage
not cowering
in fear or
trepidation
then Kali may share
Her dark wisdom
with one of
Her
children

December 21, 2012

Return Visit

returning to our cottage

after six months away

the little cottage

we fixed up together

shared for a little while

memories sweet sad

the little cottage

filled with our

intense tender love

where you disembodied

we held you as

you were leaving

you said

"I've got to get it out.

I've got to push it out.

You've got to help me get it out.

You've got to help me push it out."

I knew you were talking

about releasing your soul

your beautiful radiant

spirit body

while my mind

was not then nor now

ready to let you go

my soul agreed

to help you leave

you laid back

your beautiful

radiant soul

left your physical body

we were in shock

we sit with you

waiting for you

to breathe

again

December 22, 2012

Return Visit II

I sit here in our
bedroom
the shrine room
where you
took your
last breath
I sit in your chair
special ordered
delivered a day too late
for you to use
and cry
seven candles
are lit
at the shrine
today is the
Winter Solstice
a very sad
painful time
another Christmas
another New Years
another Chinese New Years
just over the horizon
without your physical body
I do not feel like celebrating
any of the holidays
I remember
I observe them
with intense emotion
overwhelming love

later when everyone
else goes to bed
you the goddesses
and I
will share a sip of cognac
write in our journal
and I will talk to you
you and the goddesses
drink your portion
of the cognac
very slowly
I just sip
a little
and
leave
the
rest
for
you
along
with
all
my
love

December 22, 2012

Piercing the Veil

piercing the veil

is not the correct way

not the correct image

yang image yang doing

forcing the veil to yield

embracing the veil

parting the veil

seeing beyond the veil

asking the guardian

for entrance

a wiser way

yin way yin image

yin experience

not with force

the night journey

of the soul

dreaming beyond

the veil

December 21, 2012

Holidays at Our Cottage

we moved into our little cottage
in October in time for Halloween
Thanksgiving
Winter Solstice
Christmas
New Years
Chinese New Years
your 57th birthday
fourth of July
Taryne Jade's birthday
our 33rd wedding anniversary
my birthday
we celebrated
each and every one
October 31, 2011
your beautiful radiant spirit
disembodied
your soul departed to
the spirit realm

we do not celebrate
holidays at the cottage now
there are memories everywhere
memories filled with love
often seen through tears
love bigger than anything
else

December 23, 2012

Mirror Message

not long after
your disembodiment
after a shower
the steam
clouded the mirror
I remembered
we used to
leave each
other messages
on the mirror
I drew a heart
with our initials
I put your initials first
pretending you
drew the
heart and initials
every time I shower
I would see
the message
feel your love
mixed with my
sadness for
the loss
of your
physical person

now and then
my small self
would say
"you know Carol Susan
did not draw that
on the mirror"
I would reply
"you cannot be so sure
as her finger could have
directed mine"

I clean the bathroom
but never the mirror
I do not know when I will
since
I know your finger
helped write the
message on the mirror

whenever I do clean the mirror
your finger will help write
the message again

so I guess I'll clean the
mirror
after
all

December 24, 2012

Snake Oil

Carlos was a snake oil salesman
he made his own snake oil
it contained neither snake nor oil
snake oil was not its real name
the prime ingredient is love
mixed with dreams hopes wishes
fantasies desires longings
Carlos made a bottle of amethyst crystal
carved a uroborus on each side
capped with a black rubber stopper
sealed with purple wax
Carlos made only one bottle
the snake oil was never for sale
he gave it to his beloved Susanna
already the essence of love
she always had room for more
Susanna treasured Carlos' gift of love
She removed the purple wax
black rubber stopper
charged with their love
the snake oil was vibrating

at such a high rate
it instantly transformed
into the spirit realm
Susanna laughed told Carlos
love is always in the air
as it is the mystery element
holding everything together
Susanna told Carlos
their love was beyond
space and time was
Always Forever and Beyond
Susanna and Carlos held the
bottle between them and
when they kissed
the wax stopper bottle
Susanna and Carlos
entered the spirit realm
where they remain
together
Always Forever and Beyond

rewritten December 31, 2012

Your Awareness

thinking you do not know
how hard it is for me to be
without your physical person
here with me

then I said
oh yes you know very well
you experience my distress
my missing you
my loneliness
without you near me
in your physical person

you whispered you are
painfully aware
hope I soon find the door
me too my beloved
me too

December 27, 2012 Journal IX
transcribed April 15, 2013

New Traditions

burning incense

lighting candles

writing in our journal

flowers at the shrine

writing poems

remembering

looking at our pictures

rereading the golden dreams

wearing only black

the first year

adding purple and gray

the second year

taking care of

myself like I promised

grieving

struggling with the eyes of loss

telling you things

listening to you whispering

December 29, 2012

Portal to Your Soul

when I gaze into your eyes in your picture
I am looking into your soul
you are looking back into mine
we look with eyes of love
nothing else is as real

no wonder people say
photographs steal souls
while they do not
they do provide
a portal to the spirit realm

your spirit eyes are just beyond the picture
looking into them I can see into
Always Forever and Beyond

I feel our love
am comforted
by your presence

January 1, 2013

Inexhaustible Grief

love is inexhaustible
grief appears inexhaustible too
looking from eyes of loss at
possession in great measure
eyes of loss seem to
prevail at holidays
anniversaries
birthdays
disembodiment days
eyes of love see
beyond the veil
eyes of loss see
only the physical world
as if that is all there is
my intent to see with
eyes of love
falters and weakens as
I drop into seeing with
eyes of loss
I cannot deny the reality of our loss
so sometimes I see with
eyes of love misted by eyes of loss
I know seeing with eyes of love
our love transcends
your disembodiment
but
I suspect grief may be
inexhaustible too

January 1, 2013

New Year 2013

twenty twelve
first full calendar year
without your physical person
I sit at the shrine
remembering
our New Years traditions
before your disembodiment
this New Year is different
just as was last New Years
I lit candles
burned incense across the years
remembered how we used to kiss at midnight
now I sit at the shrine
with your spirit presence
the shrine cracking in agreement
we share a sip of cognac
I kept the tradition of holding a coin or two
added the little uroborus netsuke
symbols of our union and
possession in great measure
I made buffalo chili
ate a small bowl after midnight
remembered the feasts of hors d'oeuvres
you used to make
it has been 427 days
61 weeks
since your beautiful and radiant spirit disembodied
I miss you too much
I always will

January 1, 2013

Crying

I used to tell Carol Susan
I was sorry when I started to cry
that I was not doing better
then I decided I am
doing the best that I can
I did not cry too often
before her disembodiment
I have made up for it since
now when I drop
into the eyes of loss
see from the eyes of
the Dragon Named Grief
I know crying is
no more than an
expression of my sadness
so I am not telling
Carol Susan
I am sorry for crying
quite as often
it is part of my reality
I am doing the best that I can
it is good enough for now
crying and all

January 2, 2013

Telling Carol Susan

I went grocery shopping
thinking about rewriting my story
thought I will need to include
the Dragon Named Grief
not as a hero
nor perpetrator
nor victim
nor rescuer
and the Dark Mother
Kali
in a major role
yet to be determined
I thought "I cannot wait
to get home and tell Carol Susan"
and then
I
remembered....

looked out from the eyes of the
Dragon Named Grief
again
the eyes of loss

then I remembered
I do not need to
rush anywhere to tell
my beloved
since she can hear
no matter where I am
her presence
is always with me

I still need to figure out
a transformational role
for the Dragon Named Grief
and the
Dark Mother
but somehow
after telling
Carol Susan
it is not as urgent
as before
necessary
but not
urgent

January 2, 2013

Rewriting My Story

in my story Carol Susan and I
as well as everyone who loves her
are the victims
at first the perpetrators were
the incompetent medical community
big pharma
pancreatic cancer
surgeons and oncologists
other healers
all tried to be rescuers
including me
who kept hoping for a miracle
later I blamed pollution
environmental toxicity
chemical
emotional
subtle energy
then her fragile body
then the Dark Mother
Kali
for eating my beloved
next the cruel Fates
Destiny
the Universe
for scripting
such a brief life

Carol Susan
transcended my story
by taking heroic action
disembodiment

with grace
intense love
for those
left behind
she endured
great pain
horrible treatments
to stay with her
loved ones
as long as
possible

Carol Susan
rewrote
her story

I
am
still
rewriting
mine

rewriting my story
has been a
difficult task
not seeing myself
as
victim
rescuer
nor
persecutor

I am still rewriting
my story

where I am heroic
but not a hero
a seeker but not wise
questing to rediscover
the subtle spirit realm
I visit in my dreams
paradoxically
always here
just behind the veil
even when I am
"awake"
I am
asleep
to
the subtle energy realm
the spirit realm
where stories
do not need
happy endings
since they
are
Always Forever and Beyond

January 2, 2013

written upon the occasion of reading
Alberto Villoldo. *Courageous Dreaming: How Shamans Dream the World into Being.*
Carlsbad, California: Hay House, Inc. 2008.

Dark Mother

do not contemplate
the Dark Mother
only beautiful
goddesses
of abundance
the Dark Mother
gives birth
then eats
Her children
dance of
creation destruction
life death
those who
look away
pretend they
do not see
will one day
discover
they are
Her
children
too

January 6, 2013

What Does Healing Look Like

what does healing look like
I do not know
healing the physical body
healing the emotional body
healing the mental body
healing the dreaming body
healing all the subtle bodies
healing the soul
after the disembodiment
of my soulmate

is healing
regaining
balance
equilibrium
homeostasis
becoming
accustomed
getting used to
or something else

I remember your mother Andy
used to say when asked
how she was doing
"I'm hanging in there."

later
you said the same
"I'm hanging in there."

I translated that to mean
"I feel like shit
but
I'm doing the best that I can."

I often added
a third part
to the translation

"and no one really
wants to hear about it."

not totally true
but more true
than not

what does healing look like
I do not know
I would be happy
to tell you
if I did

what does healing look like
I do not know
I'm hanging in there.

January 5, 2013

Moon Cycles

if life is
like the
cycles of
the moon
new moon=birth
waxing=youth
full=adult
waning=old age
dark moon=death
why do some
skip cycles
one of the
great mysteries
what happens
after the
dark moon
I do not know
I would tell you
if I did
you would not
believe me
anyway

January 6, 2013

written on the occasion of reading: Demetra George. *Mysteries of the Dark Moon: The Healing Power of the Dark Goddess.* New York: HarperCollins, 1992.

Negation and Mystification

deny death
look away
bad luck
to glimpse
obscure death
behind an
invisible cloud
utter platitudes
mutter condolences
move away
might be
contagious
hope you
and
yours are
not next
try not
to
think
that
way
death
may
be
listening

January 6, 2013

Carnival Rides of Grief II

my soul does not go on
the carnival rides of grief
my soul goes to the
spirit realm to be
with you
while my small self
takes another turn on
the carnival rides of grief
I want to hitch a ride
with my soul
not take any more turns on
the carnival rides of grief
I do not think
it is easy
or I would
not be taking anymore turns on
the carnival rides of grief
when I could be
beyond the veil
visiting
the spirit realm
and you

paradoxically
I am aware
I do both
at the same time

January 6, 2013

Shared Dreams

dreams I share
with you
are my life line to
spirit realm
and you
they confirm
our union
has only
changed forms
I
miss your
physical form
I have
trouble awake
seeing hearing
the spirit realm
only in
my dreams
I am
very thankful for
dreams I share
with you
my life line to
spirit realm
and
you

January 6, 2013

Missing My Kitten

Maya jumped on my lap
stretched out
started her bath
Merlin lay on
the bed watching
he stood up looking
lay down looking
I told him I
knew he missed
his little girl
being next to him
snuggling with him
I told him
I missed my little girl too
started to cry
I watched little Merlin
for a while felt bad
for him missing Maya
next to him so I
picked Maya up
put them
together
on the bed
they licked
each other
for a while
played some
went to sleep
curled up together
they are kittens
after all

I miss my
little girl
being next to me
snuggling with me
curled up together

we
are
kittens
too

January 7, 2013

Your Head On My Shoulder

I remember how much I loved
feeling you rest your beautiful
head on my shoulder
we would lay quietly
within our golden cocoon
feeling our golden love
when I remember
I get so very sad
yet from time to time
I still feel the faint energy
your beautiful spirit head
on my shoulder
from time to time

easier to remember
since you are not gone
transformed into a
different more subtle form
so I can feel your beautiful
spirit head on my shoulder
from time to time
wonderful feeling
wonderful experience
feeling our golden love
with your beautiful
spirit head on my shoulder
from time to time

January 7, 2013 Journal IX
transcribed April 15, 2013

Kittens at the Shrine

kittens
enjoy visiting the shrine
they tiptoe about
looking smelling
they know
the shrine is sacred
they do not
play with items
they smell
the purple orchid
sniff the unlit candles
Maya naps on the
double owl mola bag
sometimes Merlin too
they know
the shrine is sacred
they look at pictures
goddesses' statues images
special things
they like
to visit the shrine
pay their respects
to their
human grandmother
they know
the shrine is sacred
they are kittens
after all

January 9, 2013

Loss

having not having

holding not holding

seeing not seeing

hearing not hearing

feeling not feeling

touching not touching

smelling not smelling

tasting not tasting

cycles
of
physical
experience

beyond loss

memories dreams
love
soul's way to
Spirit
Always Forever and Beyond

January 9, 2013

Love's Shadow

grief is
love's companion

love's shadow

only a breath
heartbeat away

sometimes we forget
take love for granted
squander time

grief's companions
are regret remorse

love's shadow
is grief

January 9, 2013

Screensaver

after the
disembodiment
of my beloved
I decided
I needed to change
my screensaver
it said
"a flatland of frisky dirt"
so I changed it to
"soulmates"
then realized
that was not
totally accurate
so I changed it again to
"soulmatespiritmates"
the letters
are white and purple
on black
each time I see
my screensaver
I nod and think
yes we are
we always are
Always Forever and Beyond
my screensaver
agrees
you do too

January 9, 2013

Magic Herbs

you always dated the herbs
said they lost flavor
after a while

October 2010

last date on the herbs

one year later
your beautiful radiant spirit
left your body

now when the herbs run out
I replace the herbs in the bottles
your hands touched dated

a lot more than the herbs
have lost flavor
since you left your body

there is no harm
in having magic herbs
I know there is not
much magic to the herbs
I like to hold the bottles
your hands touched dated
the bottles have more
magic than the herbs

we both know
a lot more than the herbs
have lost flavor
since you left your body

January 20, 2013

Puppy Food

I discovered my beloved
liked corned beef hash
we tried different brands
picked one
called it
puppy food
we liked
it extra crispy
made us
smile each
time we
fixed it
puppy food
became
comfort food
for us

our daughter liked
puppy food too

after her surgery
Carol Susan could not
eat puppy food
we stopped fixing it
when she could not
share

four hundred
thirty-six days after
Carol Susan's
disembodiment
I decided to fix
some puppy food

it was ok
but not
the same
not as sweet
as when shared with
my beloved

does not
seem like
comfort food
any more

I like
remembering
when we
all ate
puppy food
together

now
puppy food
makes
me
cry

January 13, 2013

Grief's Blood
Soul's Blood

writing in our journal
language of the soul
into words
may help with healing
since I do not
know what else to do

healing is essential
being overly full of grief
makes my awareness
of the subtle realm
more difficult

so I am bleeding
some grief
onto the pages
of our journal
into poems
blood of grief
grief's blood
heart and soul blood
subtle blood too

grief's blood
grief's tears
I do not know about
grief's sweat
perhaps frustration
discouragement
despair anger
trying to make sense

of your illness
disembodiment
sweat with no results
all pain no gain

I do not hope
for mastery
beyond me

what does healing
look like
enduring
the dragon named grief
for now
working to transform
some of the energy
of grief
into the energy
needed to embrace
the spirit realm

that is what healing
looks like to me

I am not there
yet
I have hope

January 14, 2013

My Teacher

when the student is ready
the teacher will appear

1977 my teacher appeared
beautiful loving
young woman
stole my heart
shared souls
soulmates
master teacher
taught
by example
doing
kindness
thoughtfulness
caring
loving
stayed 34 years

I was a difficult student
reading processing thinking
not always appreciating
your wisdom
lessons taught
by example

I am sorry it took
your disembodiment
for me to fully appreciate
my teacher

I am very thankful
for the 34 years
even the dark times

I continue to be your student
you continue to be my teacher
I'm still learning
powered now by
grief longing missing
and
always
by
love

I am very thankful
you are still teaching me
glimpses of the spirit realm
your spirit presence
comforts me
beyond lessons
beyond learning
our love continues
the best experience
Always Forever and Beyond

January 15, 2013

No Accidents

"there are no accidents"
I do not like the phrase
rolls off the tongue too easily
offers
no compassion
no comfort
no acknowledgement
that
tragedies
loss
heartbreak
grief
occur

"there are no accidents"
ugly intellectual concept
especially when raw with grief
even if it were true
lacks compassion
another new age platitude
offers an explanation only
when the head rules the heart
there are better things to say

please do not tell the bereaved
"there are no accidents"
when they are raw with grief
offer compassion
"I am sorry for your loss"
"I do not know what to say"
"can I do anything"

sometimes words are not necessary
being with the other
may be enough
being present in silence

even if you believe
"there are no accidents"
please keep it to yourself
an act of kindness

show compassion
towards the bereaved

if
"there are no accidents"
is the best you can do
please
go
away

January 19, 2013

Old Coat

death to the body is likened
to a butterfly emerging from its cocoon
shedding the cocoon like an old coat
I understand the image of the old coat
however
even when damaged the old coat
held the soul of my beloved
which lit the old coat
with a golden radiance
even during the dark times

now the old coat
returned to ashes
stored in an urn
inscribed with
her name
dates
57 years old
the coat was not that old
I miss the old coat
no words can explain how much
the old coat was the sacred vessel
of my beloved

I know the remains of the
old coat in the urn
do not include her soul
I can still see the physical image of my beloved
feel her physical presence
the remains of the old coat a sad reminder
the butterfly emerged from the chrysalis
went home

leaving me here to grieve
remember
reaching to
connect to the
subtle spirit realm
and my beloved

the butterfly is free
returned to spirit
even though
I can feel the delicate brush
of butterfly wings
hear her soft song
subtle whispering
I still miss the old coat
the sacred vessel
of my beloved

I have never liked the image
of the old coat
I see a luminous golden chrysalis
I still love the chrysalis
sacred vessel of my beloved
it still shines
with our love
it is not inside the urn
I still see a luminous golden chrysalis
must be something wrong
with my eyes

January 23, 2013

Lilith and "Snakie's" Compassion

real story about Lilith and Adam rarely told
serpent came to Lilith offered an apple
told her about the tree of knowledge
Lilith said "well let me at it"
ate one apple after another
when she was finished she said
"OK 'Snakie' what else do you have"
"Snakie" said "well there is the fruit
from the tree of immortality
tree of eternal life"
Lilith said "hand it over"
ate her fill
Lilith realized the true nature of
serpent and herself
Lilith told "snakie" she knew
they belonged together
"Snakie" agreed
they went to a garden
of their own design

leaving Adam wondering about
alone crying
since Yahweh just finished
His handiwork
still pleased with His products
heard Adam's crying
had a rare tinge of compassion
created Eve

Lilith and "Snakie" wanted to share
their knowledge immortality
with Adam and Eve
"Snakie" returned offered an apple to Eve
she took one bite got frightened
refused to eat more
she offered the once bitten apple to
Adam who also took a bite
got frightened
refused to eat more

Lilith and "Snakie" were sad
Adam and Eve did not
eat fully from the
tree of knowledge
nor even approach the
tree of eternal life

Lilith and "Snakie" have compassion
understand
you can lead a horse to water
but you cannot make it drink
Adam and Eve were not ready
no blame compassion
another time

January 27, 2013

Lilith's Daughter Serpent's Son

Carol Susan more like Lilith than Eve
I was always – almost always-
very happy about that
occasionally her Kali aspect appeared
righteous indignation
justifiable anger
I learned improved did better
tarnish of being a son of Adam
one of the parts of my inheritance
I rejected Adam's silly shadow
appeared now and then
not often but too often
if at all
there is no counterpart to Lilith
unless it is her friend the serpent
I am more the son of the serpent
than that silly Adam
renouncing my heritage as a
son of Adam
was a big step
embracing the dragon
another

Lilith and the serpent
never left the garden
because they
made their own

January 27, 2013

One Day

one day I am going to sit watching clouds
trees
wind
sunset
moonrise
one day I am going to sit on a mountain
watching a storm in the valley below
clouds
lighting
wind
rain
one day I am going to sit at a pond
watching lotus flowers bloom
dragonflies
cranes
clouds
water
one day I am going to sit on the beach
watching the waves
ocean
tides
clouds
wind

one day when I reach middle age
retire
get older
one day…

January 26, 2013

One Day II

one day
I might remember
how to smile
again

one day
I might remember
how to laugh
again

not today

one day

when I
am older

older than
today

I know it
would be
a good sign

I can smile
and laugh
in my dreams
experience joy
visiting
the spirit realm
my beloved
special ones

one day I will
remember how to
smile again

one day I will
remember how to
laugh again

one day

not today

one day
when I am
older than today

January 26, 2013

My Healing

my healing is important
not just for me
for all of us
we are all healed
at least a little
by my healing
you because you can
worry less
our daughter because she
senses the darkness
accepts it as her own
me because I need to
be lighter to better access
the subtle energy realm
my healing is important
not just for me
for all of us
we are all healed
at least a little
by my healing

January 28, 2013 Journal IX
transcribed April 17, 2013

Our Wedding Picture

I look at our wedding picture
with such longing anguish
pain in my heart and soul
you were so young
radiant beautiful
full of life
full of love
we knew the spirit realm
experienced it together

you look like
our wedding picture now
only more radiant
more beautiful
more full of life
more full of love
I visit now and then
not nearly often enough

our wedding picture
reminds me
what is just
beyond the veil
where I visit
now and then
not nearly often enough

January 30, 2013

Family Hugs

we hugged often
merged energy created
a golden cocoon
small loving family
golden cocoon of love
best experiences of my life
golden cocoon of love
family hugs

before our daughter was born
she became part of the golden cocoon
expanded family hug
included the baby
young child
adolescent
young woman
family hugs were frequent
wonderful intense
golden cocoon of love

when my beloved became ill
family hugs became softer
not to add to the pain
love just as intense
fierce love
just more tender
sometimes the hugs
were energy bodies embracing
golden cocoon of love
family hugs

the last family hug
with my beloved's physical body
moments before she disembodied
fiercely tender
heart breakingly tender
last family hug
before my beloved wife
beloved mother
center of the family
left her physical body

family hugs are different now
part of the family has disembodied
physical body unavailable
spirit body still is
physical hugs are much softer now
spirit hugs are all the more fierce
golden energy cocoon of love
spirit family hugs
still make me cry

February 1, 2013

do or do not
there is no try
        Yoda
        Star Wars

Garden Time

when we met we recognized
our soul mates
almost right away
our higher selves knew
immediately
recognized our
golden cocoon
one of ten thousand things
golden cocoon
our garden
paradise of love
home coming
our true home
shared hearts souls

not all paradise
experienced more
garden time
than
wilderness time
when you were embodied
now garden time
called golden dreams
wilderness time
hellfires of grief
we experienced more
garden time

than wilderness time
when you were embodied

I am trying
to return to
garden time
awake
with you in your
different form
I am trying
not to try
to do
so far I am making it
complicated
difficult
my intent not absolute
or something
golden dreams
one door
other doors
stop trying to find
envision keys
garden time
golden dreams
golden cocoon
do

February 2, 2013 Journal IX
transcribed April 17, 2013

Note: My thanks to George Lukas for Star Wars Yoda quote.

I Know Very Little

I used to think I knew something about alchemy
before I experienced the hellfires of grief
I know very little
a little about the hellfires of grief

I used to think I knew something about the I Ching
before I experienced the yin side of
possession in great measure
I know very little
a little about possession in great measure

I used to think I knew something about metaphysics
before my beloved's disembodiment
I know very little
a little about tears of the heart
tears of the embodied soul
little else

setting in the alchemical crucible
hellfires of grief
the hottest fire
burning burning
burning away impurities
until what is left…
I do not know
I know very little
I'm still burning

perhaps the phoenix phenomena
rising from the ashes
perhaps constellation of the dragon

waking from the shock of horrible wounds
I do not know
I know very little

I am experiencing the hellfires of grief
dark nights of the soul
I do not know what they are teaching me
if anything
I do not know
I know very little
understand even less

I used to think I knew something
I now know
I know very little
understand even less
I am experiencing the hellfires of grief
dark nights of the soul
that much I know
otherwise
I know very little
understand even less

February 3, 2013

Shrine Balance

studying your shrine for balance
four elements earth air fire water
air is missing
metal the Asian fifth element is present
Tai Chi energies not balanced
mostly yin little yang
I have felt dark heavy
opposite of air
since your disembodiment
my focus missing yin energy
little regard for yang energy
so your shrine is out of balance
reflection of my lack of balance
not much concern until now
461 days from the
Day of Disembodiment
so I have decided to balance
the energies of the shrine
added several air elements
small air dragon
hummingbird
white owl
butterfly
small stuffed toys
bring air element lightness
to your shrine
Sacred Heart of Jesus candle
recommended
added one
yang element
added three Taoist gods

to match
three goddesses
balance of yin yang
invisible yin yang elements
better balanced too
so the shrine if more balanced
five elements yin yang
more cluttered too
sometimes some chaos
required to achieve balance
following the Emerald Tablet's
corollary statement
as within so without
balancing the shrine
a healing function
as without so within
shrine's improved balance
reflection of my own
so balancing the shrine
may seem a trivial matter
unless you know
balancing the shrine
a healing function

February 8, 2013 Journal IX
transcribed April 19, 2013

Note: My thanks to Elena Avila for her words of wisdom on balancing shrines. Elena Avila. *Woman Who Glows in the Dark: A Curandera Reveals Traditional Aztec Secrets of Physical and Spiritual Health.* New York: Tracher/Penguin, 1999.

Lunar New Year 2013

we used to celebrate
lunar new year
decorations
special food
new year's cards
talked about
Chinese zodiac
year ended
year starting
special family time
warm family tradition

then the dark times
lunar new year
year of the
black water snake
second lunar new year
since you disembodied
the year of the
black water dragon
first lunar new year
since you disembodied
image of black water
black waters of grief
black rivers of grief
black sea of grief

everyone experiences loss
black water of grief
part of human experience
does not make it easier
suddenly swept into the
dark water of grief
universal experience

who cares
trying to keep
from drowning in the
black waters of grief

lunar new year
not like before
now
lunar new year
always will be a
black water time
for me

February 10, 2013

Day of Disembodiment

Lunar New Year 2013
looking back at other
holidays celebrations
many years of warm loving memories
small family together
to the last ones
celebrated together
when you were embodied
holidays celebrations
always magical

looking at holidays celebrations
after your disembodiment
all sad pitiful events
magic went with you
Halloween saddest holiday of all
do not celebrate Halloween
turn off all the lights
burn a few candles incense
Halloween has been
transformed into the
Day of Disembodiment
day of remembering
day of loss grief
day the magic
disembodied

February 10, 2013 Journal X
transcribed April 18, 2013

Double Rainbows

out of the black waters of grief
emerges the serpent of regeneration
dragon of transformation
uroborus
glowing with the merger of
our combined energy
in our golden cocoon
rainbow bodies merging
physical bodies merging
subtle bodies merging
souls merging
spirits merging
experience of many mergers
different faces bodies
yet all one
many lives shared together
soulmates
spiritmates
always
forever
and
beyond

February 10, 2013 Journal X
Lunar New Year: Year of the Black Water Snake
transcribed February 28, 2013

High Impact Lessons

you lived from the heart
my role model teacher
sadly your lessons have higher impact now
no longer can take you even a little for granted
still think you are less accessible
mostly visit in our golden dreams
sorry I was often hard headed
much less so now
heart broken open
center dropped from my head
to my heart
difficult passage head to heart
short physical distance
drop into the void
hellfires of grief
dropped me into my heart
into the fires of grief
high impact lessons
experience of grief
intense impact
hellfires of grief
burn on and on
high impact lessons

February 10, 2013 Journal X
transcribed April 18, 2013

My Spirit Valentine

second valentine's day
since you disembodied
I miss your physical person
physical valentines 34 years
new purple orchid on your shrine
many blooms open
many yet to unfold
promise of our union
continuing to unfold
different form more subtle
I feel your love
you feel mine
valentines forever
my spirit valentine
I did not say
till death do us part
souls do not die
souls are immortal
you are my valentine
I am yours
valentines
always forever and beyond
my spirit valentine
I love you

February 13, 2013

Patience

hoping for a breakthrough
more easily part the veil
not happening discouraged
need to develop patience
impatient to develop patience
hurry up develop patience
cannot push the river
swim upstream against currents
cannot force the pace
cannot rush matters of soul
so I am slowing down
learning the pace of patience
soul's pace soul's way
my need is urgent intense
soul not to be rushed

rereading journals
extracting images for poems
slow labor intensive process
patience has taken me hostage
surrounded by necessity
developing patience
impatient to develop patience
attempt to swim upstream again
never worked before either
so I am slowing down
learning the pace of patience
soul's pace soul's way
patience soul's virtue

February 13, 2013 Journal X
transcribed April 18, 2013

Two Candles Two Flames

two candles apart
vaguely aware of the other
two flames together as one
always
candles met joined as one
two flames together as one
always
vaguely aware of many candles
in the past
in the future
two flames together as one
always
one candle remains now
knows
two flames together as one
always forever and beyond

disembodiment of my beloved
sharpened my spirit sight
more aware of two flames
many candles
two flames together as one
always forever and beyond

hard way to learn
loved the two candles together as one
miss the two candles together as one
know the two flames are together as one
always forever and beyond

February 21, 2013

Grief and Grieving

grief - a vague concept
grieving - an experience
moment by moment
memory by memory
memories triggered by
everything at first
many things later
pictures words spoken
words written stories told
items gifts cards
places
so many experiences shared
ideas images concepts
emotions feelings
dreams fantasies
music food books
love
many years together
so many roles
companions
best friends
lovers
confidants
partners
mothering ones

soulmates
spiritmates
memories of sharing
intense sharing
happy times

wonderful times
magical times
mythic times
peaceful times
joyful times
quiet times
loving times
sad times
awful times
dark times
black times
golden times

grief is a vague concept
grieving is the worst experience
of my life
moment by moment
memory by memory
memories triggered by
everything at first
many things later
I do not know
about much later
I am not there yet

February 2, 2013

Memories II

I am glad I have memories
our life shared together
intense sharing
thirty four years of sharing
memories are my closest companion
since you disembodied
I wish it were different
I wish we were making more
I am glad we shared so many experiences
so many memories of time
shared together
I cherish even the dark ones
they were shared with you

we are making new memories
strange as that may sound to some
I visit you in the spirit realm
in dreams
where we are as one
we are making new memories
in the spirit realm
I wish
I remembered
them all
I intend to

February 26, 2013

Compounded Grief

I have become vaguely aware
my grief is not only for
your disembodiment ending
thirty four years together
this lifetime
one loss awful enough
my grief is compounded by
our many lifetimes together
sometimes I disembody first
leaving my beloved behind
sometimes my beloved
disembodies first
leaving me behind

like this time

my vague awareness
of many lives together
offers some comfort
not enough
I want to escape the
wheel of time
walk hand in hand with
my beloved
into the spirit realm
never to return
my beloved agrees

February 27, 2013

Withered Up

when we first met came together
you would tell me if I did not get enough love
I would wither up like a prune
you would then announce I was starting to
look a little withered up
shower me with love
I would tell you the same
shower you with love
wonderful loving experiences
wonderful loving memories
I was very spoiled by your love
I showered you with love as well

now part of me feels withered up like a prune
the rest of me is showered by your love
when I think about your disembodiment
loss of your love
I feel withered up like a prune
when I am quiet I experience
your subtle spirit love
showering me
spoiling me with your spirit love
surrounding me always flowing
I send my love to you as well

I feel closer to the spirit realm
spoiled by your spirit love
I still get withered up like a prune
when I focus on loss
I make a strange hybrid creature
part withered up prune

part spoiled full of your spirit love
I expect part of me will always
feel withered up as long as I am embodied
more often now
I feel your spirit love
overwhelms the withering up
softens the loss
I am blessed
very thankful
for your spirit love
I am very spoiled by your spirit love
I send my love to you as well

March 3, 2013

Spirit Realm Embrace

in days gone by
we would travel together
to the spirit realm
shared spirit realm embrace
pure energy pure love
golden cocoon of love
mythology became real
beyond the mortal realm
taste of eternity
glimpse of our higher selves
soulmates together
in the spirit realm
always forever and beyond

now I travel to the spirit realm
to find you in my dreams
share spirit realm embrace
pure energy pure love
golden cocoon of love
mythology becomes real
beyond the mortal realm
taste of eternity
glimpse of our higher selves
soulmates together
in the spirit realm
always forever and beyond

now you are in the spirit realm
access seems difficult complex
except in golden dreams
yet I know the subtle spirit realm
is all around me
not far away as it seems
the veil is not external

I do not know why
it seems so dense heavy
know it is only a construct
of my small self
I do not know why
I
can not
yet
let
it
go

I intend to with
patience compassion
and perseverance
I intend to

March 3, 2013

Precious Possessions

thinking about precious possessions
your spirit presence
your love
your compassion
our golden cocoon
thirty four years embodied
together
shared experiences
awareness we knew
each other as children
many many life times together
shared golden dreams
new shared memories
your messages
whispering I sometimes hear
inspirations large and small
our healing quest
most precious possessions
are intangible

a few things are precious
we picked out together shared
gifts you gave me
precious possessions
surrounded infused with
golden energy of your love
otherwise they would be
only things

memories of our small family
precious possessions

birth of our daughter
her growing up
precious memories
precious possessions

all precious possessions
your love
your spirit presence
our golden cocoon
shared golden dreams
new memories
our healing quest
precious possessions

being with my soulmate
being with my spiritmate
most precious possessions
of all

March 6, 2013 Journal X
transcribed April 20, 2013

Sacred Clutter

looking at your shrine's
recent additions
three Taoist Gods
Sacred Heart of Jesus candle
added to balance the energy
thought your shrine
rather busy chaotic
heard you say
more clutter
I replied
but sacred clutter
you just smiled laughed
I will tidy up your shrine
before your birthday
I promise
do not know where
to put some of the
sacred clutter
will find a suitable place
right now your shrine
more reflects my
cluttered ways
than your style
so I will streamline
your shrine before
your birthday
I promise

March 4, 2013 Journal X
transcribed April 25, 2013

Two Peas in a Pod

gave you a little carving
two Asian children
boy and girl
inside a peanut shell
Asian version of
two peas in a pod
two peanuts in a shell
you liked the gift
reminds us of
being together
when small

moved the
two peanuts in a shell
to the shrine
little children
sad there needs
to be a shrine
glad to be
part of it

I am sad
there needs
to be a shrine too
glad I have one

March 11, 2013

House of Grief
Golden Angel

my golden angel
helps me wake from
my nightmare existence
golden dreams
only time I am
fully awake
I remember fragments
glimpse of spirit realm
know golden dreams
home of my higher self
long to be fully awake
another way to envision
my quest

glimpses help soften
hellfires of grief
golden dreams
shared with my beloved
helped me discover other rooms
not all are rooms of grief
at first a house of grief
all rooms alike
all rooms of grief
now I know other rooms
some elusive
discovered only in dark of night
golden dreams
physically awake
wondering room to room

hoping to find a door
hidden passage
secret panel
something
anything
then
exhausted by the search
sleep
golden dream
entrance to the spirit realm
awake in the spirit realm
golden dream
remember fragments
when I awake in
my physical body
only way so far
might have to be
enough for now

I thank my golden angel
my beloved for sharing
golden dreams

March 11, 2013

Bitter Pills

life serves nasty medicine
bitter pills to swallow
painful experiences
hard lessons
not much choice
swallow bitter pills
catch in my throat
choke them down
hard to digest
balls of emotion
harder to express
choke them down
force of will
neck pain holding in
what wants out
not what wants in
no wonder
my neck hurts
difficulty swallowing
side effects
of holding in
what wants out
bitter pills to swallow
even harder to
let go

March 4, 2013

Grieving and Conventional Wisdom

may be no wrong ways to grieve
some are healthier than others
conventional wisdom in this culture
get the deceased in the ground
as soon as possible
usually within three days
get on with your life
souls are not served by the race
to get it over past move on
attitudes values about grieving
not soulful or compassionate
grief relegated to darkest corners
of one's mind
where loss upon loss are stored
piling up higher darker thicker
heart and soul pushed aside
to observe the festering mass
constrained to act
contempt for the needs of
heart and soul
not without repercussions
may be no wrong ways to grieve
some ways are healthier than others

March 8, 2013 Journal X
transcribed April 21, 2013

Grief and Transformation

does grief work really help
I do not know
I cannot stop long enough
to find out
not like there is a choice
grief happens
and happens
and happens
some more

books say grief is transformational
I do not know
illness and disembodiment of
Carol Susan
worst experience of my life
are the hellfires of grief
dark nights of the soul
transformational
perhaps
not like being struck
by lightning on the road
one time event
may be transformational
or debilitation or both
life changing
lightning strike on the road
physical or metaphorical

loss of one's beloved is not
like being struck once by
lightning on the road
more complex complicated
small lightning strikes with
each memory
each image
extra intense lightning on special days
constant lightning storm at first
wake up with tears in my eyes
cry myself to sleep
crying even in my dreams
spirit realm much more complex
than I could ever imagine
not like being struck once by
lightning on the road
though that would certainly be
life threatening
life changing experience

at first grief is a constant
electrical storm
lightning nearly unceasing
later the storm is not as constant
lightning pauses
now and then
golden dreams
hint of rainbows forming
somewhere
not like being struck once
by lightning on the road

is grieving transformational
hell if I know
does grief work really help
hell if I know
I cannot stop long enough
to find out
not like there is a choice
grief happens
and happens
and happens
some more

almost 500 days
since the disembodiment
of my beloved
long storm
not like being struck once by
lightning on the road
before disembodiment
anticipatory grief
storms within storms
storms warning of
storms to be
storms yet to come
storms here now
almost 500 days of storms
I have been metaphorically
struck by lightning on the road
a few times

so I can tell you
grieving is nothing like that
grief happens
and happens
and happens
some more

the books say grief is transformational
I do not know
I am burning and burning
in the hellfires of grief
I know that love and loss
are the most powerful
alchemical vessels
I have experienced the golden crucible
filled with the rainbow bodies of the two
heated with the fires of love
transformed into the black crucible
containing the wounded one
left behind
heated by the hellfires of grief

so it seems I know
a little something about
transformation
after all

March 13, 2013

I Knew You As A Child

thinking about two peas in a pod
pictures of us as children
placed in the center of uroboros logo
you were two I was three
thinking about us being children
growing up separate in
time and location
then an inspiration
true we were separate
also true
I knew you as a child
before I was born
you knew me as a child
before you were born
my memory of your childhood
no clearer than my own
no photographic memory awake
I know I have always been with you in spirit
just as you have always been with me
always forever and beyond
growing up I could feel your subtle spirit
your loving compassionate presence
did not know who
or understand
now I know your presence
other half of my being
soulmates
spiritmates
always forever and beyond

March 13, 2013

Time and the Mystic

wise old man tells
young version of justice
time is only a concept
meaningless convention
artificial construct
best ignored
she laughs
come on grandfather
time to go

playing with time
turning back on itself
twisting time
bending time
the uroboros
I know time to be
if I am not careful
I could turn into a
mystic

trickster aspect
out of hiding
awake

as I have
been a mystic
all along

March 14, 2013

Five Hundred Days

five hundred days
since your beautiful and radiant spirit
left your physical body
returned to the spirit realm
five hundred days

five hundred dark nights of the soul
five hundred days and nights of tears
hellfires of grief
five hundred days

is anything special about
five hundred days
not really
grieving keeps no calendars
cares not about days
weeks months years
grieving is not about numbers
grieving is about loss
not keeping score
five hundred days

I am observing the
five hundredth day
like all the others
I might burn a little more incense
light a few more candles
sit remembering longer
cry a bit more
I got new candles
our daughter got

three purple irises
for your shrine
five hundred days

five hundred days
without your physical presence
I feel your spirit presence
your compassion
your love
surrounds me
comforts me
golden dreams
inspirations
I treasure them all
at five hundred days
I miss your physical person
I know I always will

March 17, 2013

Last Dance

you loved to dance
took classes growing up
I was not much for dancing
we rarely danced together
few months before your disembodiment
talking about our lives together
experiences good bad
talking about your regrets
you wished we had danced more together
wished we could dance right then
I played a slow song you liked
we danced about slowly
my heart breaking
I knew it was our last dance
you did too

I held you close but very softly
as we slowly danced
our last dance together
when the music stopped
you smiled said
thank you
I told you I love you
we stood holding each other
for another song or two talking softly
you said see that was not so bad
I said no it was wonderful
we both knew it was
our last dance together
I told you I was sorry we had not
danced more together
you smiled happy for the moment
last dance together in our physical bodies

I added *not dancing more*
to my list of regrets
last dance with my beloved
most tender fiercely intense love
sadness too
my beloved enjoyed the moment
so did I
even though our hearts were breaking
we knew it was our last dance together
in our physical bodies

when it is my turn to disembody
return to the spirit realm
when we meet rather than walk
hand in hand into forever
we can embrace and dance into forever
I promise

I know you find my delayed conversion
sweetly humorous
you are pleased with my eternal promise
we often dance together in my dreams
even the ones I do not remember

March 19, 2013

On Assignment

I am shocked when I want to share
something with you
when I remember happens often
the shrine sometimes jolts me into remembering
you are not working somewhere

at first
I pretended you would be coming home from
one of your consulting trips any time
I remember how happy I would be
to see you when I picked you up at the airport
you were always happy to see me too
best presents ever
you were usually tired and hungry
I was just glad you were back home
we would talk about your trip
even though we talked every day
your returning best present ever

I guess you are on a long distant assignment
working somewhere
otherwhere
I will not be meeting you at the airport
to welcome you home
the spirit realm does not need airplanes
I know you are both with me
and on assignment
otherwhere

I wish I was picking you up from the airport
bring your physical person home
you were always the best present ever
you still are

March 16, 2013

Carry Your Luggage

I planned to retire
carry your luggage
as you went from
consultation to consultation
working as your assistant
being together on the road
portable home
sadly not this time this realm
we worked together for a while
both enjoyed the experience
happy to be together
I showed potential as a facilitator
had a master teacher
another thing to add
to my list of regrets
not working together
missed opportunities
squandered time
not being able to carry your luggage
may seem like a small thing
we talked about it for years
code words for working together
almost there
just before you became ill
sad I will not be carrying your luggage
you do not need luggage
anymore

March 19, 2013

Hidden Mysteries

I have always been a seeker
convinced the mysteries are hidden
complex complicated esoteric
so I study read speculate
looking wondering about
hidden mysteries
my beloved knows the mysteries
surround us
loving embrace
soft caress
tender kiss
loving gesture
acts of loving kindness
she lived in the moment
she knows the mysteries
are not hidden
the mysteries of
life
love
we shared them together
I treasure your love
time spent together
yet I still searched
looking for
hidden mysteries
when the mysteries
were not hidden
I complicated the mysteries
while you concentrated them in a
loving embrace
soft caress

tender kiss
loving gesture
acts of loving kindness
so much compassion
so much love
I knew when we first met
you were a daughter of Tara
later added Kuan Yin and Mother Mary
multiple Mothers
different cultures same energy
people liked to be near you
even if they did not know why
feel your golden aura

while the mysteries are not hidden
they are too obvious for someone
convinced the mysteries are
complex complicated esoteric
another regret to add to my list
complicated the mysteries
so busy seeking I
squandered time
missed seeing obvious
two more regrets for the list

now my quest is to part the veil
visit the subtle spirit realm
while embodied
I wonder if this is another of the
mysteries I am complicating
I am still seeking
what was once so near
I could physically touch
surrounded by your love

ironic
simple made complex
hidden mysteries
I know I am still
surrounded by your love
golden dreams
I may be complicating the mysteries
again convinced the mysteries are hidden
while I am surrounded by your love
always forever and beyond

March 19, 2013

A Few Pitiful Poems

our lives condensed into
a few pitiful poems
many more poems
would be needed
to summarize the
good times
black times

life time of poems
would be needed
even then
pitiful summary
of our lives
our love

memories
filled with love
golden dreams
your spirit presence
comforts sustains

poems of love loss
words blood of grief
worse experience of my life
condensed into
a few pitiful poems

March 22, 2013

My Higher Self

I meet my higher self in golden dreams
I share with my beloved
even though I only meet him in my dreams
I know his presence is always with me
I call him Carlos Eldon
likely not his real name
he looks like me when I was younger
only better
I know he wears that form for me
I would recognize him anyway
by his energy
he is my teacher
guide
role model
challenging having a celestial being
role model
perhaps where my striving
seeking
touch of perfectionism
originates
good excuse as any
Carlos Eldon chuckles at my excuses
he is like my beloved
beings of compassion healers
wonderful match
always forever and beyond

yes I know
my higher self is part of my being
like a corollary to the
Emerald Tablet saying
As Above So Below
As Within So Without

I could hear my higher self whispering
from time to time
in the past he was often disguised
sometimes still is
better at recognizing and remembering
know when he visits in my dreams
tells me things I need to know
inspirations

challenge having a celestial being
role model
teacher
guide
very welcome challenge
I am grateful to remember my dream visits
with the two
they are glad
I am remembering
listening

March 20, 2013

Heart of My Heart

I gave my heart to my beloved
not my physical heart
the heart of my heart
when I found my soulmate
gave her the heart of my heart again
she gave me hers again
they fit perfectly together
as if they had always
been together
which of course
they have

we gave each other
the heart of our hearts
so long ago
I am not sure
we even had
physical hearts
back then
we had the
sacred spark of life
fire of life
heart of hearts
which we joined long ago
we recognize each other
across many life times
share the heart of our hearts
which never die
changes forms
transforms
embodies disembodies

when the physical heart
is mistaken for the
heart of hearts
the blood of love
soul's blood
changes to tears of grief
shock of losing
our physical companion
creates trauma denial
anguish grief despair
tears seem the blood of
the heart of hearts
after the loss
too raw to comprehend the
transformation
too focused on the loss of the
physical person
physical heart
to remember the
heart of hearts
is eternal
I think it is another name
for the soul

March 22, 2013

Paradox of Loss and Grief

loss and grief are universal
every one experiences loss grief

loss and grief are personal
each person's loss grief
experienced in their own way
private
individual
personal
you may see other travelers
other tourists in the hellfires of grief

dark nights of the soul
a personal journey
a private night voyage
you can sometimes recognize
others on their journey
if you look closely into their eyes
they may not welcome your stare
if fortunate you can share
take off your mask for a while
no need to say you are doing fine
share your authentic experience
both may receive a measure of comfort

paradox of loss grief
every one experiences loss grief
each in their own way
sharing all but taboo

primitive defense
trying to deny the
reality of loss grief
dying is taboo
death is taboo
grieving is taboo
very primitive attitude
why grieving is often
forced underground
not shared
too shameful
taboo
very primitive attitude
when
loss and grief are universal

March 2, 2013

Tear's Words

poems

my grief concentrated

what my tears say when I listen

my tears insisted I translate them into words

inspiration from my soul

soul's blood

been said tears are healing

not said how many

if tears are healing

perhaps tear's words

may be healing too

March 23, 2013

Golden Joy

joy went along
when you disembodied
all sizes of joy
gone with you
even the little joys
lost in the hellfires of grief
dark nights of the soul

after a while golden dreams
joy rediscovered
golden joy
first experienced when we met
golden joy went with you
returned in our
golden dreams

slowly
small joys have returned
golden dreams we share
bring golden joy
slowly small joys follow
returning only after
golden dreams
with you

March 26, 2013

Withered Up Old Dragon

I did not always feel like
a withered up old dragon
little energy little power
chakras a mess body knotted up

once upon a time I felt like a
golden rainbow dragon
unlimited energy power
kundalini awake
body supple healthy
curiosity of a large cat
my eyes seeing beauty within without
living was joyful life was good
my trickster aspect playing like a child
I did not always feel like
a withered up old dragon

what happened
many losses large and small
paper cuts to stabbing wounds
many losses many wounds
yet I had not withered up too much

then an almost fatal wound
starting with the illness of my beloved
my wound deepening with her condition
my beloved's disembodiment
cut me in two almost fatal wound
hanging on by the proverbial thread

wondering over and over why
why is my beloved gone
why am I still here
no answers

hanging on by the proverbial thread
withering up started with my beloved's illness
progressed as did her disease
sympathetic sharing
power energy eroding in the hellfires of grief
turning into a withered up old dragon

now after five hundred days
the withered up old dragon
has blinked a few times
shook his head
stretched out his body
seen himself in golden dreams
where he is the golden rainbow dragon of old
the withered up old dragon
knows he can recapture
the golden rainbow dragon of old
do not know quite how
suspect as the hellfires of grief
burn off more and more impurities
eventually the energy needed for the fire
will be reduced
energy available to empower
the withered up old dragon

the withered up old dragon
slowly awakening from the intense nightmare
worse experience of my life
will eventually regain part of the
golden rainbow dragon of old
glowing rainbow colors
radiant golden energy
the reconstituted golden rainbow dragon
will not be the same as the
golden rainbow dragon of old
the rainbow colors edged in black

half the golden rainbow dragon
in the otherwhere with my beloved
I would not have it any other way

half a golden rainbow dragon
is light years better than
a withered up old dragon
I think that is as good as
it is going to get
as my beloved liked to say
still says from time to time
it is enough

so I can tell you what healing looks like to me
healing looks like a golden rainbow dragon
I have seen him in my dreams
half will remain in the world of dreams
the other half awaken here
slowly
after all the wound was nearly fatal
hanging on by the proverbial thread
I have not always felt like
a withered up old dragon

I know hidden within the grief is
golden rainbow dragon of old
have seen him in my dreams
he has been almost fatally wounded
hanging on by the proverbial thread
slowly recovering
never to be quite the same
a deeper darker shade of rainbow
with a deeper darker golden glow
it is good enough

March 26, 2013

Destination

do not know the short term destination

am not sure of the way

do not know if I will know

when I get there

not sure it matters

if the way has heart

soul's journey

soul's destination

I know the long term destination

very well

visit in golden dreams

April 1, 2013

Experience

vicarious experience
perhaps better than none
but not by much
like reading only helps
recognize the landscape
little more
not by much
gain knowledge through
vicarious experience
knowledge leads to more knowledge
knowledge is of the mind
experience of the heart
heart of one's heart
experience may lead to wisdom
once you accumulate enough
if you are open
experience the real teacher
not knowledge

experience at times
very demanding teacher
appearing cruel ugly
my experience of the
disembodiment of my beloved
most intense teacher
I have ever experienced
classroom named grief
language spoken tears
hellfires of grief
dark nights of the soul
I do not like my grief lessons

or my teacher
does not matter
not within my control
no one considered my wishes
my teacher looks like one of the faces of
Kali
not one of Her pretty faces
Her compassion beyond my comprehension

so far beyond I assume it is
absent missing non-existent
experience a hard hard teacher
no one promised it would be another way
if someone did I can tell you
not to believe them
still surprised by how hot
the fires of grief burn
did not understand the lessons would be
so intense so painful
should not have been surprised
law of proportions
size of love
equals
size of grief
I should have known
the lessons would be
intense painful
hellfires of grief
too much vicarious experience
too much reading
not any more
I should have known
the lessons would be
intense painful

hellfires of grief
law of proportions
size of love
equals
size of grief
now I know
now I have
experience

April 1, 2013

Love

without love
no grief
for lost love

grieve for love
never found

do not ask me
which is worse

found my love
she disembodied
not lost
another form

never holding love
in your arms
never spending
years together
much worse

nothing more
cruel
than never
experiencing
love

April 5, 2013

Superficial

love and loss

joy and grief

all there

is

everything else

is

superficial

April 5, 2013

Dream Details

spent time with you
in dreams last night
do not remember
details very well
remember golden energy
glowing around us
woke up feeling very loved
which is all the memory
I really need

golden energy of
your love
surrounding me
embracing me
magic cloud
invisible to regular vision
feel with heart of hearts
golden energy
glowing around me
woke up feeling very loved
which is all the memory
I really need

April 7, 2013

Two Kinds of Seeing

faint awareness of the subtle realm
ability to be two places at once
hellfires of grief
spirit realm with you
confusing if looked at directly
too much logic
rationality hurts my head
makes my soul sick
can chose to be hyper rational
super logical
hurt my head
make my soul sick
or
chose to be in two places at once
not confusing if you look at it
from the side
sideways
crooked like
different kind of double vision
two kinds of eyes
two kinds of looking
two kinds of seeing
direct into the hellfires of grief
other into the spirit realm
second seeing works best
when I turn off my
consciousness
golden dreams
memories of my
spirit realm life
glow in the dark

I like looking sideways
crooked ways best
the excessive glare of hyper logic
super rationality
hurts my head
makes my soul sick
golden dreams
nourish my soul
comfort my grieving mind
I am very thankful for
my second kind of seeing
golden seeing
golden dreams
with you

April 9, 2013

Shocked

when I have been busy for a while
suddenly I see your shrine
really see your shrine
shocked to remember you disembodied
once again
everything stops
the dragon named grief
washes over me
once again
swallowing hard
tears leaking from my eyes
pain in the heart of my heart
shocked to remember
really remember
once again
you disembodied
five hundred twenty four days ago
hard to believe
because I do not want to
your beautiful radiant golden spirit
left your physical body
returned to the spirit realm
does not seem real
I expect you to return any minute
or to awaken from the
worse nightmare of my life
while not rational you seem to
disembody rather often
grieving on the installment plan
dragon named grief too large to swallow
so I am shocked you have disembodied
once again

April 10, 2013

Transformational Magic

I do not remember all our golden dreams
know I have them all the time
remember only a few
poor memory or
good forgetting facility
for the spirit realm
source of golden dreams
memory improves
with each golden dream
forgetting facility weakens
dragon named grief is no match
for golden dreams
grief dragon exists only on
this side of the veil
transformed on the other side
grief dragon being transformed by
golden dreams
developing faint golden glow
around the edges
perhaps will not need to eat
all the grief dragon after all
golden dreams will transform part
if I look closely
grief dragon faintly resemblances the
golden rainbow dragon
one of two who reside in golden dreams
grief dragon no match for golden dreams
golden dreams transformational magic
of the spirit realm
blessed by golden dreams

April 10, 2013

Spirit Vision

seeing into the subtle spirit realm
second sight third eye
for many of us the iron curtain drops
in early childhood
we lose the skill of seeing into
a separate reality
multidimensional sight
many of us forget we were
ever gifted with second sight
many have assistance in forgetting
ridiculed scolded
shamed punished
religions talk about angels
do not expect regular people
to see or talk to them
science applies reductionism
to everything until all that remains
is a flatland of frisky dirt
with the "frisky" part highly suspect
likely observer error
over-active imagination
non-scientific
so when sources suggest
everyone has second sight
appear to berate people who
are struggling to regain theirs
saying you are not sincere enough
do not believe that propaganda either
take heart
remember for most of us the
iron curtain fell in early childhood

between the physical world and
the subtle spirit realm
once the veil drops second sight
becomes a forgotten ability
if you have the good fortune
to retain your gift of second sight
a fully functioning third eye
count your blessings
many of us are not so blessed
most of us had assistance
in forgetting our gifts
third eyes covered with disbelief
skepticism doubts
perceptual cognitive
narrow-mindedness
some call it education
sadly for many of us the residents of
the subtle spirit realm
became invisible long ago

I always wanted to improve
my second sight
lift the veil
see into the subtle spirit realm
talked about it read studied
my interest was more curiosity
or perhaps an intuition for what
October 31, 2011
would bring
when my beloved disembodied
her beautiful radiant golden spirit
left her physical body to return
to the subtle spirit realm
my interest transformed

along with my beloved's spirit
my interest became a sacred quest
my life's new great work
my soul's purpose
loss of my beloved's physical presence
provided me with intense need
too much motivation
to seek the portal to the
subtle spirit realm
figure out how to part the veil
raise the iron curtain
open the door into a separate reality
I have been blessed my beloved and I
share golden dreams
my spirit vision
works perfect in our golden dreams
my forgetting facility is overwhelmed
by the power magic wonder majesty
of our golden dreams
the energy of golden dreams
restoring my spirit vision
slowly I remember more
forget less
undoing many years of
negative propaganda
hyper-logic
super-rationality
brain washing
not an overnight task
a sacred quest
I am blessed my beloved is
helping from the other side
her love disembodied with her spirit
continues from the spirit realm

we are together in the spirit realm
so far I only remember in a few
golden dreams
I know there is much more to
the subtle spirit realm
the golden dreams are just
a taste a sampling
the soul cannot be rushed
even though my quest is sacred
my need urgent intense
cannot force the river
I have cultivated excellent
perseverance
working to improve
patience and compassion
have an abundance of
very powerful helpers
very thankful and appreciative
for each and every one
the disembodiment of my beloved
transformed my interest in the
subtle spirit realm
from part time hobby to
my life's primary passion
my sacred quest
to regain my spirit vision
should I still be standing
when I succeed
I will tell you
what helped
regain my spirit vision
I promise

April 12, 2013

New Memories

in our journals I write how I miss
not making new memories
with you in your physical body
wish hope long ask for new memories
complain often of no new memories
with you in your physical body
rereading the thought occurred to me
how concrete my thinking
fogged by the hellfires of grief
we are making new memories
I call them golden dreams
fantastic visits with you in the spirit realm
while heartbreakingly true
we are having no new experiences
with you in your physical body
we are having wonderful experiences
golden experiences in the sacred spirit realm
I remember some when I awaken
call them golden dreams
they are golden experiences
golden memories
I miss new experiences with you
in your physical body
I am blessed we share our
spirit realm visits
new experiences
new memories
I call them golden dreams
now I call them new memories too

April 13, 2013

Little Things

miss the little things
miss them every day
sometimes one by one
sometimes in quantities
miss all the little things
about your embodied self
missing the little things
makes me sad
makes me cry
remembering the little things
warms my heart
soothes my soul
remembering the little things
makes me sad
makes me cry
not going to list the little things
far too many
many little things to miss
miss the little things
miss them every day

miss the big things too
too big for words
miss the little things
miss them every day
miss the big things too

April 14, 2013

Two Modes of Existence

thinking about all the things I treasure
about your embodied self I will always miss
no matter how wonderful the
golden dream visits to the spirit realm
experience golden dreams now and then
when not experiencing a golden dream
remembering missing your embodied self
remembering missing your subtle spirit self
I visit in golden dreams
part time in paradise
part time in the hellfires of grief
before the golden dreams
full time in the hellfires of grief
so part time in paradise
part time in hellfires of grief
progress

if I could more fully
embrace the spirit realm
two modes co-exist
paradise would transform
the hellfires of grief

I do not expect
the hellfires of grief
to go out
be reduced smaller
some grief energy transformed
would be progress
might be what healing looks like

April 14, 2013

Eighteen Months

approaching eighteen months
since your beautiful radiant spirit
disembodied
eighteen months in the hellfires of grief
worse eighteen months of my life

looking backward
asking if I have
served my experience of loss grief
active participant or passive victim
"scour my heart out with honest sorrow"
honor my experience
so my experience can serve me

sometimes yes
sometimes no
sometimes perhaps
good enough

April 15, 2013

Note: My thanks to Alberto Villoldo for the concept *serving my experience*
and to Joan Halifax for the quote "scour my heart out with honest sorrow"

Healing Journey

at first and for many months
the idea of a healing journey
described in books
other sources
irritated the hell out of me
too raw dark heavy heart broken
hemorrhaging grief
soul's blood
soul's tears
heart of my heart's blood
the idea of a healing journey
absurd
alien
trying to stay afloat
survive
achieve enough balance
to continue
my chakra cords flailing about
looking for their mates
dripping energy from their severed ends
feeling the diminished energy
in our golden cocoon
nothing felt like a
healing journey to me
hellfires of grief
burning and burning
dark nights of the soul
experienced nothing
that seemed like healing
grief CD told me I was
getting better and better

I was not
my grief was dropping lower
from my heart to my center
becoming more intense
became very irritated at the grief CD
trying to persuade brainwash
convince suggest I was getting better
as the grief became more intense
less denial dropping into the heart of grief
center of grief
image of being swallowed by
the dragon named grief
did not seem like healing to me

I did not start to heal until the
first golden dream
my beloved in her beautiful radiant
spirit form offering her love
her assistance from the spirit realm
I still did not envision a
healing journey
still too raw dark heavy heart broken
missing my beloved's embodied self
too much to care about
healing much less a journey
swallowed whole by the
dragon named grief

after more golden dreams
more time within the
dragon named grief
I became less antagonistic
towards the concept of healing
struggled to understand what

healing looks like
still not certain
continue to experience
hellfires of grief
dark nights of the soul
now can acknowledge
a healing journey
when I was riding on the
tail of the dragon named grief
there was no healing
no journey
dragon flailing about
random chaos
when I entered the
dragon named grief
started working my way through
corresponded with golden dreams
started to understand
comprehend the need to
see with eyes of love
not eyes of loss
my quest encouraged by
golden dreams
shared with my beloved
my healing conceptualized as a
journey
started to become more credible
healing journey
a lifelong process
becoming more open to the
subtle spirit realm
my beloved
the quest the healing journey
merged

improving my spirit vision
assisted by golden dreams
other experiences
lifelong process

I know what healing
looks like
feels like
experience healing in
golden dreams
remember some
when awake
blessed with golden dreams
healing journey
lifelong process

April 21, 2013

Failed Hero

traditional hero story
hero rushes in slays dragon
rescues damsel in distress
they ride off into the sunset
there must be versions
where the dragon eats the hero
damsel and the hero's horse
dragon flies off into the sunset
or waits for the next pair
I suspect failed hero
stories are all too common
who wants to tell them
who wants to hear about
failed heroes

in our story the dragon
wounds the hero
damsel disembodies
to escape cancer demons
her beautiful radiant spirit
returns to the spirit realm
so hero fails to rescue damsel
nor did any other heroes
perform a rescue miracle
failed heroes one and all
damsel's spirit never at risk
required disembodiment
for heroine to rescue herself

awful being a failed hero
when rescuing my beloved

my heart's desire
awful the way the heroine
had to rescue herself
failed hero
non-hero
not a nightmare story
not a story at all
real life experience
worse experience of my life
not a nightmare story
true life nightmare
worse experience of my life

April 24, 2013

Trio of Sad Days

April 30th eighteen months
one year and a half
since your disembodiment
May 8th fifty-ninth birthday
if still embodied
May 12th Mothers Day
Mothering Ones Day
two of the days were
not always sad
we celebrated your birthday
Mothering Ones Day
Mothers Day 34 years
this will be the second
trio of sad days
without my beloved embodied
start thinking about special days
in advance
remembering feeling sad
wishing you were still embodied
healthy
so we could celebrate the
two special days
not experience the reason
the special days have become sad
guess my wishing is flawed
wished you would get better
when you got sick
wished the surgery would
get all the cancer
wished it would never
reoccur

so now a trio of sad days
two were not always sad
days of celebration
much better times
hellfires of grief
seem hotter around special days
not that I do not miss you
every day
you know how much
just seems more intense on
special days
miss you every day
you know how much
just seems more intense on
special days

April 25, 2013

Celestial Princess

higher self recognized you instantly
known you all along
always forever and beyond
smaller self took longer to discover
somewhere around thirty days
by then you had stolen my heart
you did not even need to try
freely gave it to you
along with my soul
smaller self figured out
what my higher self knew all along
embodied Celestial Princess
my soulmate embodied
intensely miss my
embodied Celestial Princess
still my Celestial Princess
visit in shared golden dreams
higher self known you all along
always forever and beyond
small self envious
only remembers some
golden dreams
higher self lives in the
golden spirit realm
with my Celestial Princess
wish my small self
could remember better
more golden dreams
more visits with my
Celestial Princess

April 24, 2013

Eighteen Months II

nearing eighteen months since
your beautiful radiant spirit disembodied
time of remembering looking back
wonderful loving times
dark times then black times
struggling with hellfires of grief
want to look into the beyond
metasenses impaired
constant complaint
golden dreams portal into beyond
only remember a few
perhaps the others are
too radiant to remember
more aware of your spirit presence
your subtle energy
your subtle love

golden dreams
your subtle love
slowly transforming grief dragon
radiance too much for grief dragon
slow progress
patience perseverance compassion
eighteen long months
eighteen sad months
eighteen black months
worse eighteen months of my life

April 27, 2013

Birthday Present 2013

if still embodied
you would be 59 this birthday
I observe your birthdays
since you disembodied
very hard days
your birthdays were always
very special days
when you were embodied
I was so happy to share
them with you
planned your presents
months in advance
this year your present
collection of 222 grief poems
I wrote for you
we know they are love poems too
our love transcends physical realm
so your birthday present this year
collection of grief poems
we know they are love poems too
even if the emphasis is grief and loss
still love poems
love always forever and beyond

April 27, 2013

little irrational

been replenishing our flatware
buying missing pieces now and then
bit strange
replenishing our flatware
magical thinking
restore everything to like
when everything was new
physical realm as radiant
as spirit realm
when we first met
golden cocoon paradise
know replenishing our flatware
has no magic to perform
a restoration miracle
does not mean I will not try
know it is irrational
do not care does no harm
tell myself our daughter
will enjoy the flatware
used it all her life
has emotional value
rationalization to excuse
my irrational restoration miracle
friend said everybody's
little irrational early in grieving
know it is true
later is true for me too
do not care does no harm

April 28, 2013

Sweet Sweet Attention

Merlin jumped on top
bathroom cabinet
immediately started to cry
to be rescued
got him down
held him close
rubbed on him
told him he did not
get enough attention
which is untrue
told him I used to get
lots of attention too
sweet sweet attention
you always spoiled me
painfully aware how much
now your physical being is gone
I miss your sweet sweet attention
know I always will
I miss your physical being
know I always will

April 28, 2013

Sweet Sweet Attention II

missing your attention
partial truth
your spirit presence surrounds me
your attention unceasing
not easy for me to perceive
your subtle spirit being
difficult to directly encounter
sense your presence
my metasenses impaired
determined to improve
refine my metasenses
stop whining
constant complaining
expand our contact

golden dreams
vague sense perceptions
tired of my whining
constant complaining
know you and
old alchemist are too

April 28, 2013

Missing Your Physical Being

you became the center of my life
soon after we met
your disembodiment has not
changed that
you continue to be the
center of my life
even more intense
since I can no longer
see your physical being
my grief acknowledges
my love and loss
recognizes your impact on my life
empty space where your
physical being used to be
still the center of my life
trying to fill it with memories
ceremonies poems
words in our journal
seeing with eyes of loss
know your spirit presence
can over flow the empty space
where your physical being used to be
if only I can look with eyes of love
focus on my spirit realm blessings
rather than my physical realm losses
simple in theory
memory of your intense love
spoiling me when you were
physically embodied
know I spend too much time
looking with eyes of loss
today is week seventy-eight
tomorrow eighteen months
next your birthday

Mother's Day
Mothering One's Day
focus on
missing your physical being
seeing with eyes of loss

I am working to see primarily with
eyes of love
with as much intensity of focus
intent will that I can manifest
my quest requires
patience perseverance compassion
I am improving
slowly
confident I will successfully
realize my quest
lots of helpers
helps when I perceive
your spirit presence filling
up the huge space where
your physical being used to be
golden cocoon continues
to be beautiful radiant
when seen with eyes of love

missing your physical being
know I always will
helps to perceive your
spirit presence filling up
the void where
your physical being used to be
golden cocoon beautiful radiant
seen with eyes of love

April 29, 2013

Energy Bodies
Energy Connections

we have multiple energy bodies
all have energy connections
to multiple energy bodies
of those we love
greater the love
more and stronger
energy connections
when ones beloved
disembodies
lower energy bodies reabsorbed
lower energy connections severed
all other subtle energy bodies
energy connections
remain
spark of life vacates physical body
lower energy bodies reabsorbed
lower energy connections severed
what many call death
loss of physical being
lower energy bodies
lower energy connections
of one's beloved
what I prefer to call
disembodiment
when beautiful radiant spirit
returns to the spirit realm
worse experience of my life

at first I thought
my beloved's half of our
shared golden cocoon
was empty
looking with eyes of loss
lost physical being
lost lower energy bodies
lost lower energy connections
when I was able to look
with eyes of love
discovered all the other
subtle energy bodies
all the other
energy connections
are still there
using the wrong kind of seeing

loss of physical being
loss of lower energy bodies
loss of lower energy connections
worse experience of my life
hellfires of grief
dark nights of my soul

sensed my beloved's half
shared golden cocoon
not empty
her physical being
lower energy bodies
lower energy connections
no longer present
my beloved's spirit presence
unchanged
her half of golden cocoon

filled with subtle energy
my beloved's subtle spirit presence
golden dreams shared with
my beloved
helped me to see with
eyes of love
golden cocoon
beautiful radiant as ever
seeing with spirit vision
still see with eyes of loss
more and more often
seeing with eyes of love
spirit vision
most energy bodies
most energy connections
are
always forever and beyond

April 30, 2013

Note: References include Barbara Ann Brennan *Hands of Light: A Guide to Healing Through the Human Energy Field* and *Light Emerging: The Journey of Personal Healing* and others.

Looking Back
Looking Beyond

spend a lot of time remembering
looking back reminiscing
warm loving memories
dark memories
black memories
spend a lot of time looking back
part of the landscape of loss
hellfires of grief
spend some time looking forward
brief glimpses of progress
on my quest
to look into beyond
sacred spirit realm
where I most want to look
brief glimpses
golden dreams
into beyond
where I most want to look
suspect the way
not as complicated
as I think it needs to be
sacred spirit realm
all around
just do not know how to see
just do not know how to look
yet

April 29, 2013

My Grief and I Ching

question: how to cope with my loss
two changing lines
first hexagram 56 The Wanderer
image fire on the mountain
wanderer moves from place to place
transitional state limited progress
grieve over the loss you have suffered
fire hellfires of grief
mountain size of grief
changes to hexagram 32 Duration
image of thunder over wind
long duration
storms of grief
develop perseverance endure
remain true to your inner resolve
to follow the soul's path

January 10, 2012
transcribed April 26, 2013

Reference:
Richard Wilhelm (translation) Cary F Baynes (English translation). **The I Ching or Book of Changes, Volume I**. London: Routledge and Kegan Paul, Ltd., 1951.

My Quest and I Ching

question: how to pursue my quest
changing line
first hexagram 48 The Well
image water above wood below
nourishment spiritual wisdom
inexhaustible well
spring of the divine
danger if can not
drink water of life
cut off from spiritual nourishment
neglect self development
no progress
changes to hexagram 39 Obstruction
image abyss before mountain behind
obstructions means difficulties
retreat yield turn inward
gather strength
seek inspiration from higher self
cultivate spirit development
perseverance brings good fortune

March 3, 2012
transcribed April 26, 2013

Reference:
Richard Wilhelm (translation) Cary F Baynes (English translation). **The I Ching or Book of Changes, Volume I**. London: Routledge and Kegan Paul, Ltd., 1951.

My Path and I Ching

question: does my path need adjustment
two changing lines
first hexagram 49 Revolution-Molting
image fire above lake below
eliminate what is no longer needed
make necessary changes
change brings revolution
starting brings good fortune
changes to hexagram 39 Power of the Great
image thunder in heaven above
perseverance furthers
wise to continue on the
soul's path
success is certain

July 31, 2012
transcribed April 26, 2013

Reference:
Richard Wilhelm (translation) Cary F Baynes (English translation). **The I Ching or Book of Changes, Volume I**. London: Routledge and Kegan Paul, Ltd., 1951.

Making Room

experience a void in my life
where your physical presence
used to be
try to fill the void with memories
reminiscences looking back
hold good memories tightly
until I miss you too intensely
then dark memories
black memories intrude
know I need to make room
for your spirit presence
looking with eyes of love
seeing with the heart
experience the void already filled
with your spirit presence
your spirit love
looking with eyes of love
seeing with the heart
making room for your
spirit presence
experience the void already filled
with your spirit love

May 1, 2013

Making Room II

cleaned up your shrine
put away many things
put away sacred clutter
many memories attached
know tidying up your shrine
metaphor for putting away memories
shrine's clutter symbolic of
clutter of many memories
not enough room for new memories
new experiences
focused on the past
past experiences
memories reminisces
remembering longing
shrine still a sacred place
filled with memories
past experiences
with my beloved
more room now for new experiences
new memories
open space
blank space
did not wipe the past clean
achieved a measure of balance
difficult putting away each special item
each one connected to many memories
many experiences with my beloved
time to make room for new memories
experiences into beyond

collection of poems
another way to honor
our past experiences
memories of our embodied lives together
completing the 222 poems
another way of making room
for new experiences
new memories
into beyond
my quest to embrace the spirit realm
my beloved
now there is better balance
less clutter
more room

May 3, 2013

Golden Cocoon Waiting

golden cocoon had been waiting
our higher selves together
always forever and beyond
when our physical beings met
golden cocoon embraced us
physical realm spirit realm
merged
universe pleased we found
each other again
universe conspired to
reunited us again
destiny fate kismet
exceptional pure magic
miracle of love
reentry into paradise
rediscovery of our soulmate
spiritmate
always forever and beyond

I wish everyone the extreme good
fortune of finding their soulmate
my soulmate wishes the same
physical realm would be
a much better place

April 30, 2013

Healing Broken Hearts

we have multiple energy bodies
multiple energy centers
lower energy bodies
lower energy centers
most impacted by
disembodiment of my
beloved
multiple broken hearts
multiple hearts split in two
energy hemorrhage at first
then healing started
too raw dark heavy
to see golden hands
holding multiple broken hearts
holding two halves together
golden love
golden energy
golden hands
healing my multiple broken hearts
holding them together
taken me 18 months
to see what healing looks like
golden hands
holding my broken hearts together
very appreciative
for my beloved's
golden hands

May 3, 2013

Making Room III

I have discovered dwelling in the past
provides comfort mixed with pain of loss
makes missing your physical being
more intense
when I focus on our spirit realm
togetherness
our golden love becomes the center
your physical being was the center
for 34 years
so making room a gradual process
awakening to the healing of
your spirit presence
making room not easy
setting aside 34 years of memories
physical realm
experiences shared good dark
black golden
love shared
making room for new
golden experiences
making room for new
golden memories
our spirit realm golden love
always forever and beyond

May 4, 2013

Make the Best of It

very wise teacher recently told me
I need to make the best of what I have
situation I find myself in
resources available
my skills attributes limitations
need to make the best of what I am given
very hard school
very hard lessons
I have wanted to improve
my spirit vision
as you say from time to time
"be careful what you wish for"
so my indiscriminate wishing
has resulted in my having to
make the best of it
I am very sorry I was not
more careful in my wishing
now I am going to have to
make the best of it

May 4, 2013

Fresh Eyes New Eyes

you facilitated people learning
to see with "fresh eyes" new eyes
different ways of seeing
new ways of looking
during the last years
I have seen horrible things
with my old eyes
your illness horrible treatments
your disembodiment
anticipatory grief turning to grief
hellfires of grief
dark nights of the soul
struggling seeing with old eyes
then golden dreams
your spirit presence
beautiful radiant golden spirit
seeing with fresh eyes new eyes
your golden rainbow spirit
facilitating my seeing
fresh eyes new eyes
improving my spirit vision
your facilitation continues
always forever and beyond
not surprised
very appreciative
for your facilitating
my improved spirit vision
seeing with new eyes fresh eyes
very sorry for the terrible cost
as a wise teacher told me
I am making the best of your facilitation

May 4, 2013

Making the Best of It

making the best of it
alchemical process
hellfires of grief
burn off impurities
transform gross matter
refine condense
way to
golden rainbow dragon
pair of golden rainbow dragons
have glimpses
golden dreams
other experiences
improved spirit vision
gradual transformation
reality of our loss unchanged
intensely miss your
physical being
our physical realm
togetherness
dark nights of the soul
hellfires of grief
continue burning and burning
slow painful process
gradual transformation
still I am certain
I am making the best of it
my beloved and the old alchemist
agree are pleased

May 5, 2013

Inspiration

horrible my inspiration
your disembodiment
most awful experience
cannot wake up from this nightmare
realize I already had the golden land
beside me all along
now you are no longer
so easy to see

I guess my hide was too thick for
anything else to have impact
compelled to write
poems good bad awful
just need to be out
sometimes I look at them
as if aliens
where in hell
then I remember
my inspiration
hellfires of grief
awful kind of inspiration

it is not that I did not treasure you
for I certainly have
always forever and beyond
sometimes I squandered time
written this down many times
guess not near enough
like a scene from after school
little boy at the blackboard writing
I will not squander time
over and over
I do not think it helps
all that much

mostly a petty punishment
not meeting my own
expectations
paradoxically writing down
I will not squander time
over and over
squanders time

awful horrible way to
gain inspiration
alien poems from hell
unfortunately I know too well
source of inspiration
hellfires of grief
emptiness in my life
your physical person used to fill
all the poems in the world
could never fill the void

only takes one
golden dream

golden dreams
my real inspirations

poems
only squandering time

March 6, 2013

Poems and I Ching

at one hundred poems wondered
if they might be of value to others
assist others dealing with
their hellfires of grief
translate tears of grief into words
images concepts
poems do not change loss
provide crude map
grief's awful frightening ugly landscape
measure of recognition
ointment for grief's wounds
perhaps healing energy

so decided to consult the I Ching
pose the question changing lines
first hexagram 55 Abundance
image of thunder and lightening
clarity within   movement without
time of understanding
changes to second hexagram
56 The Wanderer
image of fire on the mountain
success through smallness
I Ching seems to suggest small success
increased clarity understanding
good enough

February 17, 2013 Journal X
transcribed April 22, 2013

Reference: Richard Wilhelm (translation) Cary F. Baynes (English translation). ***The I Ching or Book of Changes, Volume 1.*** London: Routledge and Kegan Paul, Ltd. 1951.

Gone Not Gone

physical body three lower energy bodies
devastatingly gone lost missing
leaving at least six subtle energy bodies
subtle energy centers remaining
I miss the four gone lost absent
easiest to perceive with my
regular senses
poorly developed metasenses
very appreciative for what remains
very appreciative for what is gone
two truths
paradox of loss no loss
gone not gone
physical realm loss
spirit realm no loss
subtle spirit realm being
unconstrained by
physical realm limitations
spirit realm energy bodies
always forever and beyond
joyful truth
physical realm body
lower energy bodies gone
painful truth
helps to know
paradox of two truths
need spirit vision
to see to know
spirit realm truth

April 30, 2013

Hellfires of Grief II

no end to love
no end to loss
no end to grief
while embodied
hellfires of grief
burn on and on
little less raw
some impurities burned away
words in our journals
few pitiful poems
bleeding off some heaviness
little less heavy
chakra cords leak energy
looking for their mates
energy hemorrhage
until golden dreams
less energy leakage
sweetness joy magic
went with you
until golden dreams
transform darkness
little less dark
dragon named grief
slowly being transformed
by golden dreams
your golden spirit presence
golden radiance of your love
even with impaired metasenses
I know you are present
hellfires of grief
hottest alchemical fire

human body psyche
can endure embodied
grieving on the installment plan
healing on the installment plan too
golden dreams
your golden spirit presence
golden radiance of your love
transforming the grief dragon
no end to love
no end to loss
no end to grief
while embodied
hellfires of grief
burn on and on
little less raw
little less heavy
little less dark
hellfires of grief healing
coexist
healing journey
into the hellfires of grief
grief dragon
healing journey
hellfires of grief
coexist
no end to love
no end to loss
no end to grief
while embodied

April 25, 2013

Carol Susan 2013

1977

numinous power of the Feminine

natural expression of mysterious Yin ways

primal archetypal image of Woman

essence of flowering lotus

enchanting mythological princess

beautiful daughter of Tara

transformation's Divine Vessel

from you I see my changing

you guide by being you

you are also changing

we are becoming friends

2013

soulmates
spiritmates
always forever and beyond

C. Eldon Taylor
March 27, 2013

March 27, 1977 – March 27, 2013
36 years

Quotations Appendix

1. Joan Halifax. ***Being with Dying: Cultivating Compassion and Fearlessness in the Presence of Death.*** Boston: Shambhala, 2009

"When my mother died, I realized one of the hardest and most precious teachings of my entire life. I realized that I only had this one chance to grieve her death. I felt like I had a choice. On the one hand, I could be a so-called 'good Buddhist,' accept impermanence, and let go of my mother with great dignity. The other alternative was to scour my heart out with honest sorrow. I chose to scour. …I sank back into shadows of sorrow…. And my sadness became part of the river of grief that pulses deep inside us, hidden from view but informing our lives at every turn."
(page 192)

Life and death are of supreme importance.
Time passes swiftly and opportunity is lost.
Let us awaken
      awaken….
Do not squander your life.
      Zen Night Chant   (page196)

2. Elisabeth Kubler-Ross and David Kessler. ***On Grief and Grieving: Finding the Meaning of Grief Through the Five Stages of Loss.*** New York: Scribner, 2005.

"The stages have evolved since their introduction, and they have been very misunderstood over the past three decades. They were never meant to help tuck messy emotions into neat packages. They are responses to loss

that many people have, but there is not a typical response to loss, as there is not typical loss. Our grief is an individual as our lives.
The five stages – denial, anger, bargaining, depression, and acceptance – are part of the framework that makes up our learning to live with the one we lost. They are tools to help us frame and identify what we may be feeling. But they are not stops on some linear timeline in grief. Not everyone goes through all of them or goes in a prescribed order." (page 7)

"...grief is not a project with a beginning and an end. It is a reflection of a loss that never goes away. We simply learn to live with it, both in the foreground and in the background. Where grief fits in our lives is an individual thing, often based on how far we have come in integrating the loss....You don't ever bring the grief over a loved one to a close." (page 158)

"The reality is that you will grieve forever. You will not 'get over' the loss of a loved one; you will learn to live with it. You will heal, and you will rebuild yourself around the loss you have suffered. You will be whole again, but you will never be the same. Nor should you be the same, nor would you want to." (page 230)

3. Robert Bly and Marion Woodman. ***Maiden King: The Reunion of Masculine and Feminine.*** New York: Henry Holt and Company, 1998.

"How Kali Belongs in the Malls"
"...The Mall of America in Minneapolis it the largest mall in the world, and it has a statue of Snoopy taller than any statue of Christ in Minneapolis. If we replaced Snoopy with a statue of Kali, with her fangs, her bloody cleaver, her necklace of skulls, her long tongue hanging out, we would

see the true face of mall culture. Everyone who saw it would be a tiny bit more adult....
...So the image of Kali as an Eater helps people to become adult..." (page 69 by Robert Bly)

"...suddenly a shining one crosses our path. Whether that one comes in vision or in flesh, for one moment we are whole as we have never been whole before. We love. We carry the possibility of being loved.... He recognizes his soul.... she initiates in him the Warrior energy to fight for what is precious to him. Those 'Moments of Dominion/That happen on the Soul' change life. In a flash, all the best that is in us connects and flashes through and, especially when we are young, is projected outward onto that One who carries our soul. All that we never imagined within us is born. The archetypal voltage, turned up full, flows through us so that ordinary life suddenly has beauty and meaning. We are alive. Many of us can remember such a moment – a moment that shone..." (Marian Woodman pages 161-162)

4. Thomas Moore. *The Reinchantment of Everyday Life*. New York: HarperCollins, 1996.

" a shrine is a means of making visible that which is invisible and for evoking a presence that is otherwise only vaguely sensed." (page 288)

5. Thomas Moore. *Soul Mates: Honoring the Mysteries of Love and Relationship*. New York: Harper Collins, 1994

"To outward appearances, endings are a structural matter- now there is a relationship, now there is not relationship. From the soul point of view, ending is a different experience of the relationship. Ending is not literal at all, but is rather a radical shift in imagination. ...

In this respect it is important to honor the dead, especially those with whom we have a close relationship. The soul is not limited in its experience to the confinements of life. Death doesn't erase a relationship, it simply places it in a different context. Fostering our relationships to the dead gives the soul its nourishment of eternity, melancholy, mystery, and the kind of relatedness that is not literally of this world. Many, many stories of the soul tell that is not fully at home in this life and that it is always trying to break the bonds of this world's limitations. We can honor the soul by nurturing our relationships with the dead, whether by visiting and decorating their graves, by praying for them when their memories drift into mind, by naming our children after them, by preserving and using objects they've left behind, or by telling their stories and keeping photographs and paintings of them within sight. ...

One radical difference between care of soul and a great deal of modern psychological work is that the former offers a profound appreciation for the personalities who are important in our lives, even if they are flawed people and even if the relationship is not perfect. Psychology prefers to analyze with the goal of increased understanding, yet understanding does little for the soul. Imagine telling stories of the dead, not for insight into ourselves, but simply to establish a deep, continuing relationship with them. The soul is given eternity in that exchange, while understanding offers it little more that another fragment of logic that has nothing to do with establishing a home for the infinite within our finite lives.

It isn't a question, anyway, of deciding whether we should or should not give attention to the dead. They present themselves to us in unsought memories, in dreams, and in momentary visitations during the day or night. ... (pages 200-203)

We can be initiated and educated by moments of torment, if only we place a flower at its shrine, or spill some wine to honor that very place in our intimacy that has been painfully opened for our contemplation and attention. (page 229)

6. Marie-Louise Von Franz. ***Alchemy: An Introduction to the Symbolism and the Psychology.*** Toronto: Inner City Books, 1980.

"'He extinguishes the fire in its own inner measure.'...the fire has to burn the fire, one just has to burn in the emotion till the fire dies down and becomes balanced. That is something which unfortunately cannot be evaded. The burning of the fire, of the emotion, cannot be tricked out of one's system; there is no recipe for getting rid of it, it has to be endured. The fire has to burn until the last unclean element has been consumed, which is what all alchemical texts say in different variations, and we have not found any other way either. It cannot be hindered but only suffered till what is mortal or corruptible, or as our text says so beautifully, till the corruptible humidity, the unconsciousness, has been burnt up. That is the meaning, it is the acceptance of suffering. ...Sitting in Hell and roasting there is what brings forth the philosopher's stone; as it is said here, the fire is extinguished with its own inner measure." (pages 252 and 254)

7. Brennan, Barbara Ann. ***Hands of Light: A Guide to Healing Through the Human Energy Field***. New York: Bantam Books, 1988.

Chakra cords: "Whenever a person creates a relationship with another human being, cords grow between the two 3A chakras. (solar plexus) The stronger the connection between the two people, the stronger and greater in number these cords will be. In cases where a relationship is ending, the cords are slowly disconnected. Cords develop between other chakras of people in relationships also……through this center, (heart chakra) we connect cords to heart centers of those with whom we have a love relationship…. You probably heard the term 'heartstrings,' which refers to these cords." (pages 75-76)
Death: "…the lower three bodies were breaking up…" (etheric, emotional, mental) "The lower three chakras were also breaking up…" (base/root, sacral, solar plexus) (page 68)

8. Brennan, Barbara Ann. ***Light Emerging: The Journey of Personal Healing***. New York: Bantam Books, 1993.

"Since the cords are connected on the fourth level of the field and higher, which exists before and beyond three-dimensional physical space, many cord connections actually occur before life in the physical dimension begins. They continue to exist even after the death of anyone involved. The cords remain connected to the deceased people, who have left their bodies and are in the astral or spiritual world. Once they are made, these cord connections never cease. They never dissolve. They are beyond the physical world. At physical death, the auric field of the fourth level and higher doesn't really go through much of a change. It simply isn't connected to a physical body anymore. Therefore, it is not surprising that the cord connections remain after physical death.

...The fuller and stronger the relationship, the fuller and stronger the cords. The more interactions in a relationship, the more cords for that relationship. The more relationships we create the more cords we create.

...In intimate, long-term relationships, we build many cords that connect us through all our chakras. It is in this way we build very deep intimate relationships and remain psychically connected to people no matter where they are on earth, and no matter how much time has elapsed since seeing them.

...One of the most painful experiences in life is to lose a loved one through abandonment, divorce, or death. The cords usually get badly damaged in these experiences. I have seen all the chakras on the front of the body torn open, with the cords floating out in space, after such trauma. The personal experience of such a trauma is described as the feeling of being torn apart, or as if their better half is missing. Many people become disoriented and don't know what to do with themselves."
(pages 184, 186)

9. Dion Fortune ***Through the Gates of Death*** (1930) republished as ***Dion Fortune's Book of the Dead.*** Boston: Weiser Books, 2005.

"It may seem like a strange thing to say, but true love is not emotional in its nature, but is an attitude of the soul towards life. True love is a spiritual radiation, like sunlight... To those who are united in spirit, death is but a temporary severance. There must be loneliness, and there

must be burdens to be shouldered alone that were once shared by the other, but there is not that sense of spiritual annihilation which devastates those who have laid up their treasure where moth and rust corrupt. It is this inner certainty of an enduring bond which is the sheet-anchor in times of bereavement....When there is a real tuning of two souls, they are literally together on the Inner Planes, where to be of one mind is to be of one place....if there is a true spiritual union we remain in touch, wherever our bodies may be....the bond of spiritual union survives all severance whether of space or time and continues to inspire and to protect both of those who are held in its tie, upon what ever plane they may be...This spiritual communion continues uninterruptedly through the death of the body and all the after death experiences of the soul...When spiritual love is coming to us from the Inner Planes we have only to still the outer senses for a moment to hear it purling like the brook, a steady flow, coming to us all the time from the eternal and steadfast soul that has gone ahead to the Next Country. And we on our side, if we still love, may send out an equally steady flow to comfort our beloved."
(pages 24-26)

Copyright Acknowledgement Permissions

I wish to thank the publishers who granted permission to reprint excerpts from the following:

from *Alchemy: An Introduction to the Symbolism and the Psychology* by Marie-Louise von Franz, ©1980 by Marie-Louise von Franz. Reprinted by permission of INNER CITY BOOKS.

from *Being with Dying: Cultivating Compassion and Fearlessness in the Presence of Death* by Joan Halifax, ©2008 by Joan Halifax. Reprinted by permission of Shambhala.

from *Soul Mates: Honoring the Mysteries of Love and Relationship* by Thomas Moore, ©1994 by Thomas Moore. Reprinted by permission of HarperCollins.

from *The Reinchantment of Everyday Life* by Thomas Moore, ©1996 by Thomas Moore. Reprinted by permission of HarperCollins.

from *Dion Fortune's Book of the Dead* by Dion Fortune, ©1995, 2000 by Society of Inner Light, London. Reprinted by permission of Redwheel/Weiser.

from *Maiden King: The Reunion of Masculine and Feminine* by Robert Bly and Marion Woodman, ©1998 by Robert Bly and Marion Woodman. Reprinted by permission of Henry Holt.

from *Hands of Light: A Guide to Healing Through the Human Energy Field* by Barbara Ann Brennan, ©1987 by Barbara A. Brennan. Reprinted by permission of Bantam Books/Random House.

from *Light Emerging: The Journey of Personal Healing* by Barbara Ann Brennan, ©1993 by Barbara Ann Brennan. Reprinted by permission of Bantam Books/Random House.

from *On Grief and Grieving: Finding the Meaning of Grief Through the Five Stages of Loss* by Elisabeth Kubler-Ross Family Limited Partnership and David Kessler Inc., ©2005 by Elisabeth Kubler-Ross and David Kessler. Reprinted by permission of Scribner/SimonSchuster.

Acknowledgements

Celestial Helpers-Healers:
Carol Susan, Carlos Eldon, and others

Embodied Helpers-Healers:
Carol Susan, Carlos Eldon, Taryne Jade, Denise Conner, Maya and Merlin, Johanna Moorman, Carol Pollock, Nancy Powell, Deb Cannon, Alice Claussen, Dede Dancing, and others

Taylor DeVaney Wong Family Support:
Especially Taryne Jade, Bob, Martha, Itzel, Manuela, Mater, Doris, Diana, Carmen and Alfonso, Fanny and Tommy, Ceci, Chicho, and others

Author

C. Eldon Taylor is a psychotherapist licensed as a Licensed Professional Counselor (LPC – Virginia), Licensed Mental Health Counselor (LMHC – Florida), and National Certified Counselor. None of which was much help when it became his turn to experience the hellfires of grief and dark nights of the soul after the disembodiment of his beloved Carol Susan.

Contact Information:
celdontaylor@gmail.com

I welcome your comments about your experiences reading *Hellfires of Grief: Love Poems*.
I will recommend resources and reference information upon request. The information will be limited to what I have found helpful.

www.ingramcontent.com/pod-product-compliance
Lightning Source LLC
Chambersburg PA
CBHW032059090426
42743CB00007B/172